D1627126

WITHDRAWN

894.3513   c.1

NAZIM HIKMET.
    SELECTED POETRY.

1986   9.95   12-89

Alameda Free Library
Alameda, California

WITHDRAWN

In praise of the Blasing/Konuk translations of Nazim Hikmet:

"The little hitherto obtainable in English of Nazim Hikmet's poetry, as well as all I have ever heard and read about his life, has always filled me with joy, hope, and new determination towards poetry and struggle. Of how many poets, even among those one admires, can one say that? How good to have this volume of convincing translations, with its excellent and moving introduction! I would like to see Hikmet's work have a wide audience here and become—as it may—a profound influence on American poets."   —DENISE LEVERTOV

"The first time I read Hikmet's *On Living* I wept because the poem released something in me, opened me to a strange and ancient happiness. Like those moments in Chekhov's stories that reach into you and cure, Hikmet's work has the healer's touch. And this version is a masterpiece—with Rexroth's *Tu Fu,* Arrowsmith's *Pavese,* Waley's *Po Chu-I*— these are many of the most overwhelming poems in English. I, you, everybody stands up in Hikmet's poems, fully mortal, compassionate, earthly, amazed, openly what we are, unashamed, in favor of life. We better listen: this is one moral and emotional vision we desperately need."   —STEPHEN BERG

"Such a poet as Hikmet is beyond our hopes in this country. He is pure feeling. He writes our most private thoughts with a zest and love that makes us treasure them in ourselves. We learn to love ourselves through love of him, a poet who bestrides the world of man ever joyfully, even in dwelling upon his sorrows."   —DAVID IGNATOW

"Hikmet is one of the few important political poets of the century because politics and revolution are more than ideological weapons in his work; they are elements in a language of love which holds closely and passionately to the simplest acts of living. We are lucky to have these fine lucid translations."   —PAUL ZWEIG

"The book certainly should be welcomed. Hikmet is clearly a figure of great energy and talent...many of these are a real addition to contemporary poetry in English."   —W.S. MERWIN

NAZIM HIKMET
Selected Poetry

Translated by Randy Blasing and Mutlu Konuk

PERSEA BOOKS
New York

c.1

ALAMEDA FREE LIBRARY

894.3513
NAZIM HIKMET

The contents of this book originally appeared, in somewhat different form, in *The American Poetry Review, The Denver Quarterly, Literature East and West, Poetry East,* and *Poetry Now* and in two earlier books, *Things I Didn't Know I Loved* (Persea, 1975) and *The Epic of Sheik Bedreddin* (Persea, 1977).

Copyright © 1986 by Randy Blasing and Mutlu Konuk
All rights reserved.

For information, contact:
Persea Books, Inc.
225 Lafayette Street
New York, New York 10012

Library of Congress Cataloging-in-Publication Data

Nazim Hikmet, 1902-1963.
  Selected poetry.

  (Persea series of poetry in translation)
  I. Blasing, Randy. II. Konuk, Mutlu, 1944-
III. Title. IV. Series.
PL248.H45A23   1986   894'.3513   86-16944
ISBN 0-89255-101-1 (pbk.)

The publication of this book has been supported in part by a grant from the National Endowment for the Arts.

Printed in the United States of America
First Edition
Typesetting by Keystrokes, Lenox, Mass.

ALAMEDA FREE LIBRARY

CONTENTS

INTRODUCTION

NAZIM HIKMET, popularly recognized and critically acclaimed in Turkey as the first and foremost modern Turkish poet, is known around the world as one of the great international poets of the twentieth century, and his poetry has been translated into more than fifty languages. Born in 1902 in Salonika, where his father was in the foreign service, Hikmet grew up in Istanbul. His mother was an artist, and his pasha grandfather wrote poetry; through their circle of friends Hikmet was introduced to poetry early, publishing his first poems at seventeen. He attended the Turkish naval academy, but during the Allied occupation of Istanbul following the First World War, he left to teach in eastern Turkey. In 1922, after a brief first marriage ended in annulment, he crossed the border and made his way to Moscow, attracted by the Russian Revolution and its promise of social justice. At Moscow University he got to know students and artists from all over the world. Hikmet returned to Turkey in 1924, after the Turkish War of Independence, but was soon arrested for working on a leftist magazine. In 1926 he managed to escape to Russia, where he continued writing poetry and plays, met Mayakovsky, and worked with Meyerhold. A general amnesty allowed him to return to Turkey in 1928. Since the Communist Party had been outlawed by then, he found himself under constant surveillance by the secret police and spent five of the next ten years in prison on a variety of trumped-up charges. In 1933, for example, he was jailed for putting up illegal posters, but when his case came to trial, it was thrown out of court for lack of evidence. Meanwhile, between 1929 and 1936 he published nine books—five collections and four long poems—that revolutionized Turkish poetry, flouting Ottoman literary conventions and introducing free verse and colloquial diction. While these poems established him as a new major poet, he also published several plays and novels and worked as a bookbinder, proofreader, journalist, translator, and screenwriter to support an extended family that included his second wife, her two children, and his widowed mother.

Then in January 1938 he was arrested for inciting the Turkish armed forces to revolt and sentenced to twenty-eight years in prison on the grounds that military cadets were reading his poems, particularly *The Epic of Sheik Bedreddin*. Published in 1936, this long poem based on a fifteenth-century peasant rebellion against Ottoman rule was his last book to appear in Turkey during his lifetime. His friend Pablo Neruda relates Hikmet's account of how he was treated after his arrest: "Accused of attempting to incite the Turkish navy into rebellion, Nazim was condemned to the punishments of hell. The trial was held on a warship. He told me he was forced to walk on the ship's bridge until he was too weak to stay on his feet, then they stuck him into a section of the latrines where the excrement rose half a meter above the floor. My brother poet felt his strength failing him. The stench made him reel. Then the thought struck him: my tormentors are keeping an eye on me, they want to see me drop, they want to watch me suffer. His strength came back with pride. He began to sing, low at first, then louder, and finally at the top of his lungs. He sang all the songs, all the love poems he could remember, his own poems, the ballads of the peasants, the people's battle hymns. He sang everything he knew. And so he vanquished the filth and his torturers."* In prison, Hikmet's Futurist-inspired, often topical early poetry gave way to poems with a more direct manner and a more serious tone. Enclosed in letters to his family and friends, these poems were subsequently circulated in manuscript. He not only composed some of his greatest lyrics in prison but produced, between 1941 and 1945, his epic masterwork, *Human Landscapes*. He also learned such crafts as weaving and woodworking in order to support himself and his family. In the late Forties, while still in prison, he divorced his second wife and married for a third time. In 1949 an international committee, including Pablo Picasso, Paul Robeson, and Jean-Paul Sartre, was formed in Paris to campaign for Hikmet's release, and in 1950

Memoirs, trans. Hardie St. Martin (New York: Penguin, 1978), pp. 195–96.

he was awarded the World Peace Prize. The same year, he went on an eighteen-day hunger strike, despite a recent heart attack, and when Turkey's first democratically elected government came to power, he was released in a general amnesty.

Within a year, however, he was drafted—at forty-nine—for military service in Korea; leaving his wife and infant son, he fled Turkey in a small fishing boat and was rescued by a Romanian freighter in the Black Sea. Taken to Moscow, he was given a house in the writers' colony of Peredelkino outside the city; the Turkish government denied his wife and child permission to join him. Although he suffered a second heart attack in 1952, Hikmet traveled widely during his exile, visiting not only Eastern Europe but Rome, Paris, Havana, Peking, and Tanganyika: "I traveled through Europe, Asia, and Africa with my dream / only the Americans didn't give me visa." Stripped of his Turkish citizenship in 1959, he chose to become a citizen of Poland, explaining he had inherited his blue eyes and red hair from a Polish ancestor who was a seventeenth-century revolutionary. In 1959 he also married again. The increasingly breathless pace of his late poems—often unpunctuated and, toward the end, impatient even with line divisions—conveys a sense of time accelerating as he grows older and travels faster and farther than ever before in his life. During his exile his poems were regularly printed abroad, his *Selected Poems* was published in Bulgaria in 1954, and generous translations of his work subsequently appeared there and in Greece, Germany, Italy, and the USSR. He died of a heart attack in Moscow in June 1963.

After his death, Hikmet's books began to reappear in Turkey; in 1965 and 1966, for example, more than twenty of his books were published there, some of them reprints of earlier volumes and others works appearing for the first time. The next fifteen years saw the gradual publication of his eight-volume *Collected Poems*, along with his plays, novels, letters, and even children's stories. At the same time, various selections of his poems went through multiple printings, and numerous biographies and critical studies of his poetry were published. But except for brief periods between 1965 and 1980, his work has been suppressed in his native country for the past half century. Since his death, major translations of his poetry have continued to appear in England, France, Germany, Greece, Poland, Spain, and the United States; for example, Yannis Ritsos's Greek versions had gone through eight printings as of 1977, and Philippe Soupault's 1964 "anthology" was reissued in France as recently as 1982. And in 1983 alone, new translations of Hikmet's poems were published in French, German, and Russian. A collection of Hikmet's finest shorter poems in English translation, this book brings together for the first time—in substantially revised new versions—the better part of two earlier selections, the long-out-of-print *Things I Didn't Know I Loved* and *The Epic of Sheik Bedreddin*, as well as a number of important lyrics previously published in magazines but hitherto uncollected.

Like Whitman, Hikmet speaks of himself, his country, and the world in the same breath. At once personal and public, his poetry records his life without reducing it to self-consciousness; he affirms the reality of facts at the same time that he insists on the validity of his feelings. His human presence or the controlling figure of his personality—playful, optimistic, and capable of childlike joy—keeps his poems open, public, and committed to social and artistic change. And in the perfect oneness of his life and art, Hikmet emerges as a heroic figure. His early poems proclaim this unity as a faith: art is an event, he maintains, in social as well as literary history, and a poet's bearing in art is inseparable from his bearing in life. The rest of Hikmet's life gave him ample opportunity to act upon this faith and, in fact, to deepen it. As Terrence Des Pres observes, Hikmet's "exemplary life" and "special vision"—"at once historical and timeless, Marxist *and* mystical"—had unique consequences for his art: "Simply because in his art and in his person Hikmet opposes the enemies of the human spirit in harmony with itself and the earth, he can speak casually and yet with a seriousness that most modern American poets never dream of attempting."* In a sense, Hikmet's prosecutors honored him by believing a book of poems could incite the military to revolt; indeed, the fact that he was persecuted attests to the credibility of his belief in the vital importance of his art. Yet the suffering his faith cost him—he never compromised in his life or art—is only secondary to the suffering that must have gone into keeping that faith. The circumstances of Hikmet's life are very much to the point, not only because he continually chose to remain faithful to his vision, but also because his life and art form a dramatic whole. Sartre remarked that Hikmet conceived of a human being as something to be created. In his life no less than in his art, Hikmet forged this new kind of person, who was heroic by virtue of being a creator. This conception of the artist as a hero and of the hero as a creator saves art from becoming a frivolous activity in the modern world; as Hikmet's career dramatizes, poetry is a matter of life and death.

Mutlu Konuk

*"Poetry and Politics: The Example of Nazim Hikmet," *Parnassus* 6 (Spring/Summer 1978): 12, 23.

Early Poems

GIOCONDA AND SI-YA-U

to the memory of my friend SI-YA-U,
whose head was cut off in Shanghai

A CLAIM

Renowned Leonardo's
world-famous
"La Gioconda"
has disappeared.
And in the space
vacated by the fugitive
a copy has been placed.

The poet inscribing
the present treatise
knows more than a little
about the fate
of the real Gioconda.
She fell in love
with a seductive
graceful youth:
a honey-tongued
almond-eyed Chinese
named SI-YA-U.
Gioconda ran off
after her lover;
Gioconda was burned
in a Chinese city.

I, Nazim Hikmet,
authority
on this matter,
thumbing my nose at friend and foe

five times a day,
undaunted,
claim
I can prove it;
if I can't,
I'll be ruined and banished
forever from the realm of poesy.

1928

Part One
Excerpts from Gioconda's Diary

15 March 1924: Paris, Louvre Museum

At last I am bored with the Louvre Museum.
You get fed up with boredom very fast.
I am fed up with my boredom.
And from the devastation inside me
    I drew this lesson:
        to visit
           a museum is fine,
        to be a museum piece is terrible!
In this palace that imprisons the past
I am placed under such a heavy sentence
that as the paint on my face cracks out of boredom
I'm forced to keep grinning without letting up.
Because
    I am the Gioconda from Florence
whose smile is more famous than Florence.
I am bored with the Louvre Museum.
And since you get sick soon enough
        of conversing with the past,
I decided
    from now on
to keep a diary.
Writing of today may be of some help
        in forgetting yesterday . . .
However, the Louvre is a strange place.
Here you might find
Alexander the Great's
    Longines watch complete with chronometer,
but
not a single sheet of clean notebook paper

or a pencil worth a piaster.
Damn your Louvre, your Paris.
I'll write these entries
                on the back of my canvas.
And so
when I picked a pen from the pocket
of a nearsighted American
                sticking his red nose into my skirts
—his hair stinking of wine—
                                I started my memoirs.
I'm writing on my back
        the sorrows of having a famous smile . . .

18 March: Night

The Louvre has fallen asleep.
In the dark, the armless Venus
                looks like a veteran of the Great War.
The gold helmet of a knight gleams
as the light from a night watchman's lantern
                                strikes a dark picture.
Here
        in the Louvre
                my days are all the same
                        like the six sides of a wood cube.
My head is full of sharp smells
        like the shelf of a medicine cabinet.

20 March

I admire those Flemish painters:
is it easy to give the air of a naked goddess
                                to the plump ladies

of milk and sausage merchants?
But
     even if you wear silk panties,
cow + silk panties = cow.

Last night
     a window
          was left open.
The naked Flemish goddesses caught cold.
All day
today,
     turning their bare
mountain-like pink behinds to the public,
            they coughed and sneezed . . .
I caught cold, too.
So as not to look silly smiling with a cold,
I tried to hide my sniffles
            from the visitors.

1 April

Today I saw a Chinese:
     he was nothing like those Chinese with their topknots.
How long
     he gazed at me!
I'm well aware
     the favor of Chinese
          who work ivory like silk
            is not to be taken lightly . . .

11 April

I caught the name of the Chinese who comes every day:
            SI-YA-U.

16 April

Today we spoke
in the language of eyes.
He works as a weaver days
and studies nights.
Now it's a long time since the night
came on like a pack of black-shirted Fascists.
The cry of a man out of work
who jumped into the Seine
rose from the dark water.
And ah! you on whose fist-size head
                  mountain-like winds descend,
at this very minute you're probably busy
building towers of thick, leather-bound books
to get answers to the questions you asked of the stars.
READ
SI-YA-U
     READ ...
And when your eyes find in the lines what they desire,
                  when your eyes tire,
rest your tired head
              like a black-and-yellow Japanese chrysanthemum
                     on the books ...
                     SLEEP
                        SI-YA-U
                           SLEEP ...

18 April

I've begun to forget
the names of those fat Renaissance masters.

I want to see
        the black bird-and-flower
                                watercolors
            that slant-eyed Chinese painters
                                        drip
            from their long thin bamboo brushes.

NEWS FROM THE PARIS WIRELESS

        HALLO
                HALLO
                        HALLO
        PARIS
                PARIS
                        PARIS...
Voices race through the air
                like fiery greyhounds.
The wireless in the Eiffel Tower calls out:
        HALLO
                HALLO
                        HALLO
        PARIS
                PARIS
                        PARIS...

"I, TOO, am Oriental—this voice is for me.
My ears are receivers, too.
I, too, must listen to Eiffel."
News from China
            News from China
                        News from China:
The dragon that came down from the Kaf Mountains
                        has spread his wings
across the golden skies of the Chinese homeland.
But
in this business it's not only the British lord's

gullet shaved
   like the thick neck
      of a plucked hen
that will be cut
but also
   the long
     thin
       beard of Confucius!

FROM GIOCONDA'S DIARY

21 April

Today my Chinese
    looked me straight
       in the eye
and asked:
"Those who crush our rice fields
   with the caterpillar treads of their tanks
and who swagger through our cities
   like emperors of hell,
are they of YOUR race,
   the race of him who CREATED you?"
I almost raised my hand
   and cried "No!"

27 April

  Tonight at the blare of an American trumpet
—the horn of a 12-horsepower Ford—
      I awoke from a dream,
and what I glimpsed for an instant
      instantly vanished.
What I'd seen was a still blue lake.

In this lake the slant-eyed light of my life
          had wrapped his fingers around the neck of a gilded fish.
I tried to reach him,
my boat a Chinese teacup
and my sail
              the embroidered silk
                      of a Japanese
                            bamboo umbrella . . .

NEWS FROM THE PARIS WIRELESS

          HALLO
                    HALLO
                            HALLO
          PARIS
                    PARIS
                            PARIS
The radio station signs off.
Once more
                blue-shirted Parisians
                        fill Paris with red voices
                        and red colors . . .

FROM GIOCONDA'S DIARY

2 May

Today my Chinese failed to show up.

5 May

Still no sign of him . . .

8 May

My days
             are like the waiting room
                             of a station:
eyes glued
            to the tracks . . .

10 May

Sculptors of Greece,
painters of Seljuk china,
weavers of fiery rugs in Persia,
chanters of hymns to dromedaries in deserts,
dancer whose body undulates like a breeze,
craftsman who cuts thirty-six facets from a one-carat stone,
and YOU
             who have five talents on your five fingers,
                      master MICHELANGELO!
Call out and announce to both friend and foe:
because he made too much noise in Paris,
because he smashed in the window
                      of the Mandarin ambassador,
           Gioconda's lover
                      has been thrown out
                                      of France . . .
My lover from China has gone back to China . . .
And now I'd like to know
who's Romeo and Juliet!
If he isn't Juliet in pants
                      and I'm not Romeo in skirts . . .
Ah, if I could cry—
                      if only I could cry . . .

12 May

Today
when I caught a glimpse of myself
in the mirror of some mother's daughter
touching up the paint
on her bloody mouth
in front of me,
the tin crown of my fame shattered on my head.
While the desire to cry writhes inside me
I smile demurely;
like a stuffed pig's head
my ugly face grins on...
Leonardo da Vinci,
may your bones
become the brush of a Cubist painter
for grabbing me by the throat—your hands dripping with paint—
and sticking in my mouth like a gold-plated tooth
this cursed smile...

Part Two
The Flight

Ah, friends, Gioconda is in a bad way . . .
Take it from me,
        if she didn't have hopes
                of getting word from afar,
she'd steal a guard's pistol,
             and aiming to give the color of death
to her lips' cursed smile,
             she'd empty it into her canvas breast . . .

FROM GIOCONDA'S DIARY

O that Leonardo da Vinci's brush
had conceived me
                under the gilded sun of China!
That the painted mountain behind me
had been a sugar-loaf Chinese mountain,
that the pink-white color of my long face
                     could fade,
that my eyes were almond-shaped!
And if only my smile
            could show what I feel in my heart!
Then in the arms of him who is far away
         I could have roamed through China . . .

FROM THE AUTHOR'S NOTEBOOK

I had a heart-to-heart talk with Gioconda today.
The hours flew by
             one after another

like the pages of a spell-binding book.
And the decision we reached
will cut like a knife
                    Gioconda's life
                              in two.
Tomorrow night you'll see us carry it out...

FROM THE AUTHOR'S NOTEBOOK

The clock of Notre Dame
                    strikes midnight.
Midnight
          midnight.
Who knows at this very moment
          which drunk is killing his wife?
Who knows at this very moment
          which ghost
                    is haunting the halls
                              of a castle?
Who knows at this very moment
          which thief
                    is surmounting
                              the most unsurmountable wall?
Midnight... Midnight...
Who knows at this very moment...
I know very well that in every novel
                    this is the darkest hour.
Midnight
          strikes fear into the heart of every reader...
But what could I do?
When my monoplane landed
                    on the roof of the Louvre,
the clock of Notre Dame
                    struck midnight.
And, strangely enough, I wasn't afraid

as I patted the aluminum rump of my plane
                        and stepped down on the roof...
Uncoiling the fifty-fathom-long rope wound around my waist,
I lowered it outside Gioconda's window
like a vertical bridge between heaven and hell.
I blew my shrill whistle three times.
And I got an immediate response
to those three shrill whistles.
Gioconda threw open her window.
This poor farmer's daughter
                        done up as the Virgin Mary
chucked her gilded frame
and, grabbing hold of the rope, pulled herself up...

SI-YA-U, my friend,
                you were truly lucky to fall
to a lion-hearted woman like her...

FROM GIOCONDA'S DIARY

This thing called an airplane
                        is a winged iron horse.
Below us is Paris
        with its Eiffel Tower—
                a sharp-nosed, pock-marked, moon-like face.
We're climbing,
                climbing higher.
Like an arrow of fire
                we pierce
                        the darkness.
The heavens rise overhead,
                        looming closer;
the sky is like a meadow full of flowers.
                We're climbing,
                        climbing higher.

. . . .
. . . .
. . . .

I must have dozed off—
                I opened my eyes.
Dawn's moment of glory.
The sky a calm ocean,
our plane a ship.
I call this smooth sailing, smooth as butter.
Behind us a wake of smoke floats.
Our eyes survey blue vacancies
                    full of glittering discs. . .
Below us the earth looks
                  like a Jaffa orange
                        turning gold in the sun. . .
By what magic have I
                  climbed off the ground
                      hundreds of minarets high,
and yet to gaze down at the earth
                  my mouth still waters. . .

FROM THE AUTHOR'S NOTEBOOK

Now our plane swims
                within the hot winds
                    swarming over Africa.
Seen from above,
                Africa looks like a huge violin.
I swear
they're playing Tchaikovsky on a cello
                  on the angry dark island
                        of Africa.
And waving his long hairy arms,
                a gorilla is sobbing. . .

We're crossing the Indian Ocean.
We're drinking in the air
           like a heavy, faint-smelling syrup.
And keeping our eyes on the yellow beacon of Singapore
—leaving Australia on the right,
           Madagascar on the left—
and putting our faith in the fuel in the tank,
           we're heading for the China Sea. . .

*From the journal of a deckhand named John aboard a
British vessel in the China Sea*

One night
    a typhoon blows up out of the blue.
Man,
    what a hurricane!
Mounted on the back of a yellow devil, the Mother of God
        whirls around and around, churning up the air.
And as luck would have it,
        I've got the watch on the foretop.
The huge ship under me
    looks about this big!
The wind is roaring
    blast
        after blast,
           blast
             after blast. . .
The mast quivers like a strung bow.(*)

———————

(*)What business do you have being way up there?
    Christ, man, what do you think you are—a stork?
                 N.H.

Oops, now we're shooting sky-high—
　　　　　　　my head splits the clouds.
Oops, now we're sinking to the bottom—
　　　　　　　my fingers comb the ocean floor.
We're leaning to the left, we're leaning to the right—
that is, we're leaning larboard and starboard.
My God, we just sank!
　　　　　　Oh no! This time we're sure to go under!
The waves
leap over my head
　　　　　　like Bengal tigers.
Fear
　　leads me on
　　　　　　like a coffee-colored Javanese whore.
This is no joke—this is the China Sea...(*)

Okay, let's keep it short.
PLOP...
What's that?
A rectangular piece of canvas dropped from the air
　　　　　　　into the crow's nest.
The canvas
　　　　was some kind of woman!
It struck me this madame who came from the sky
　　　　　would never understand
　　　　　　our seamen's talk and ways.
I got right down and kissed her hand,
　　and making like a poet, I cried:
"O you canvas woman who fell from the sky!
Tell me, which goddess should I compare you to?
Why did you descend here? What is your large purpose?"

————

(*)The deckhand has every right to be afraid.
　　The rage of the China Sea is not to be taken lightly.
　　　　　　　　N.H.

31

She replied:
"I fell
        from a 550-horsepower plane.
My name is Gioconda,
        I come from Florence.
I must get to Shanghai
                as soon as possible."

FROM GIOCONDA'S DIARY

    The wind died down,
            the sea calmed down.
The ship makes strides toward Shanghai.
The sailors dream,
            rocking in their sailcloth hammocks.
A song of the Indian Ocean plays
            on their thick fleshy lips:
"The fire of the Indochina sun
warms the blood
            like Malacca wine.
They lure sailors to gilded stars,
            those Indochina nights,
                those Indochina nights.

Slant-eyed yellow Bornese cabin boys
knifed in Singapore bars
paint the iron-belted barrels blood-red.
Those Indochina nights, those Indochina nights.

A ship plunges on
to Canton,
55,000 tons.
Those Indochina nights. . .

As the moon swims in the heavens
    like the corpse of a blue-eyed sailor
        tossed overboard,
Bombay watches, leaning on its elbow...
                Bombay moon,
                   Arabian Sea.
The fire of the Indochina sun
warms the blood
    like Malacca wine.
They lure sailors to gilded stars,
           those Indochina nights,
              those Indochina nights..."

Part Three
Gioconda's End

Shanghai is a big port,
an excellent port.
Its ships are taller than
horned mandarin mansions.
My, my!
What a strange place, this Shanghai...

In the blue river boats
with straw sails float.
In the straw-sailed boats
naked coolies sort rice,
                        raving of rice...
My, my!
What a strange place, this Shanghai...

Shanghai is a big port.
The whites have tall ships,
the yellows' boats are small.
Shanghai is pregnant with a red-headed child.
My, my!

FROM THE AUTHOR'S NOTEBOOK

Last night
when the ship entered the harbor
Gioconda's foot kissed the land.
Shanghai the soup, she the ladle,
she searched high and low for her SI-YA-U.

"Chinese work! Japanese work!
Only two people make this—
a man and a woman.

Chinese work! Japanese work!
Just look at the art
in this latest work of LI-LI-FU."

Screaming at the top of his voice,
the Chinese magician
                    LI.
His shriveled yellow spider of a hand
tossed long thin knives into the air:
one
        one more
                    one
                        one more
                                five
                                    one more.
Tracing lightning-like circles in the air,
six knives flew up in a steady stream.
Gioconda looked,
            she kept looking,
                    she'd still be looking
but, like a large-colored Chinese lantern,
            the crowd swayed and became confused:
"Stand back! Make way!
Chiang Kai-shek's executioner
                    is hunting down a new head.
Stand back! Make way!"

One in front and one close behind,
two Chinese shot around the corner.

The one in front ran toward Gioconda.
The one racing toward her, it was him, it was him—yes, him!
Her SI-YA-U,
            her dove.
                  SI-YA-U...
A dull hollow stadium sound surrounded them.
And in the cruel English language
            stained red with the blood
                  of yellow Asia
                        the crowd yelled:
"He's catching up,
he's catching up,
            he caught—
                  catch him!"

Just three steps away from Gioconda's arms
Chiang Kai-shek's executioner caught up.
His sword
            flashed...
Thud of cut flesh and bone.
Like a yellow sun drenched in blood
SI-YA-U's head
                  rolled at her feet...
And thus on a death day
Gioconda of Florence lost in Shanghai
her smile more famous than Florence.

FROM THE AUTHOR'S NOTEBOOK

A Chinese bamboo frame.
In the frame is a painting.
Under the painting, a name:
                  "La Gioconda"...
In the frame is a painting:
      the eyes of the painting are burning, burning.

In the frame is a painting:
        the painting in the frame comes alive, alive.
And suddenly
        the painting jumped out of the frame
                as if from a window;
                        her feet hit the ground.
And just as I shouted her name
she stood up straight before me:
        the giant woman of a colossal struggle.

She walked ahead,
        I trailed behind.
From thẽ blazing red Tibetan sun
to the China Sea
                we went and came,
                we came and went.
I saw
        Gioconda
                sneak out under the cover of darkness
through the gates of a city in enemy hands;
I saw her
in a skirmish of drawn bayonets
                strangle a British officer;
I saw her
at the head of a blue stream swimming with stars
wash the lice from her dirty shirt. . .

Huffing and puffing, a wood-burning engine
dragged behind it
forty red cars seating forty people each.
The cars passed one by one.
In the last car I saw her
standing watch:
                a frayed lambskin hat on her head,
                        boots on her feet,
                        a leather jacket on her back. . .

Ah, my patient reader!
Now we find ourselves in the French
military court in Shanghai.
The bench:
four generals, fourteen colonels,
and an armed black Congolese regiment.
The accused:
Gioconda.
The attorney for the defense:
an overly crazed
—that is, overly artistic—
                    French painter.
The scene is set.
                    We're starting.

The defense attorney presents his case:

"Gentlemen,
this masterpiece
        that stands in your presence as the accused
is the most accomplished daughter of a great artist.
Gentlemen,
        this masterpiece...
Gentlemen...
My mind is on fire...
Gentlemen...
        Renaissance...
Gentlemen,
        this masterpiece—
                twice this masterpiece...
Gentlemen, uniformed gentlemen..."

"C-U-U-U-T!
        Enough.
Stop sputtering like a jammed machine gun!
Bailiff,
        read the verdict."

The bailiff reads the verdict:

"The laws of France
        have been violated in China
by the above-named Gioconda, daughter of one Leonardo.
Accordingly,
        we sentence the accused
                to death
                        by burning.
And tomorrow night at moonrise,
a Senegalese regiment
                will execute said decision
                        of this military court. . ."

THE BURNING

Shanghai is a big port.
The whites have tall ships,
the yellows' boats are small.
A thick whistle.
                A thin Chinese scream.
A ship steaming into the harbor
                capsized a straw-sailed boat. . .
Moonlight.
Night.
Handcuffed,
        Gioconda waits.
Blow, wind, blow. . .

A voice:
"All right, the lighter.
Burn, Gioconda, burn. . ."
A silhouette advances,
a flash. . .
They lit the lighter
and set Gioconda on fire.
The flames painted Gioconda red.
She laughed with a smile that came from her heart.
Gioconda burned laughing. . .

Art, Shmart, Masterpiece, Shmasterpiece, And So On,
    And So Forth,
        Immortality, Eternity—
                            H-E-E-E-E-E-E-E-E-E-Y. . .

    "HERE ENDS MY TALE'S CONTENDING,
    THE REST IS LIES UNENDING. . ."
                            THE END

                                        1929

LETTER TO MY WIFE

11-11-33
Bursa Prison

My one and only!
Your last letter says:
"My head is throbbing,
                my heart is stunned!"
You say:
"If they hang you,
            if I lose you,
                        I'll die!"
You'll live, my dear—
my memory will vanish like black smoke in the wind.
Of course you'll live, red-haired lady of my heart:
in the twentieth century
                grief lasts
                        at most a year.

Death—
a body swinging from a rope.
My heart
            can't accept such a death.
But
you can bet
        if some poor gypsy's hairy black
                    spidery hand
                        slips a noose
                            around my neck,
they'll look in vain for fear
                    in Nazim's
                        blue eyes!
In the twilight of my last morning
I
will see my friends and you,

and I'll go
to my grave
            regretting nothing but an unfinished song...

My wife!
Good-hearted,
golden,
eyes sweeter than honey—my bee!
Why did I write you
                they want to hang me?
The trial has hardly begun,
and they don't just pluck a man's head
                        like a turnip.
Look, forget all this.
If you have any money,
                buy me some flannel underwear:
my sciatica is acting up again.
And don't forget,
a prisoner's wife
            must always think good thoughts.

HYMN TO LIFE

The hair falling on your forehead
                       suddenly lifted.
Suddenly something stirred on the ground.
The trees are whispering
                   in the dark.
Your bare arms will be cold.

Far off
        where we can't see,
               the moon must be rising.
It hasn't reached us yet,
        slipping through the leaves
               to light up your shoulder.
But I know
        a wind comes up with the moon.
The trees are whispering.
Your bare arms will be cold.

From above,
from the branches lost in the dark,
               something dropped at your feet.
You moved closer to me.
Under my hand your bare flesh is like the fuzzy skin of a fruit.
Neither a song of the heart nor "common sense"—
before the trees, birds, and insects,
my hand on my wife's flesh
              is thinking.
Tonight my hand
            can't read or write.
Neither loving nor unloving...
It's the tongue of a leopard at a spring,
                   a grape leaf,
                      a wolf's paw.

To move, breathe, eat, drink.
My hand is like a seed
                    splitting open underground.
Neither a song of the heart nor "common sense,"
neither loving nor unloving.
My hand thinking on my wife's flesh
                            is the hand of the first man.
Like a root that finds water underground,
it says to me:
"To eat, drink, cold, hot, struggle, smell, color—
not to live in order to die
but to die to live..."

And now
as red female hair blows across my face,
as something stirs on the ground,
as the trees whisper in the dark,
and as the moon rises far off
                    where we can't see,
my hand on my wife's flesh
before the trees, birds, and insects,
I want the right of life,
of the leopard at the spring, of the seed splitting open—
                    I want the right of the first man.

1937

Poems from Prison

LETTERS FROM A MAN IN SOLITARY

1
I carved your name on my watchband
with my fingernail.
Where I am, you know,
I don't have a pearl-handled jackknife
(they won't give me anything sharp)
           or a plane tree with its head in the clouds.
Trees may grow in the yard,
but I'm not allowed
               to see the sky overhead. . .
How many others are in this place?
I don't know.
I'm alone far from them,
they're all together far from me.
To talk to anyone besides myself
              is forbidden.
So I talk to myself.
But I find my conversation so boring,
         my dear wife, that I sing songs.
And what do you know,
that awful, always off-key voice of mine
        touches me so
              that my heart breaks.
And just like the barefoot orphan
     lost in the snow
in those old sad stories, my heart
—with moist blue eyes
and a little red runny nose—
          wants to snuggle up in your arms.
It doesn't make me blush
        that right now
           I'm this weak,
              this selfish,
                this *human* simply.

No doubt my state can be explained
physiologically, psychologically, etc.
Or maybe it's
           this barred window,
               this earthen jug,
                   these four walls,
               which for months have kept me from hearing
               another human voice.

It's five o'clock, my dear.
Outside,
           with its dryness,
               eerie whispers,
                       mud roof,
and lame, skinny horse
       standing motionless in infinity
—I mean, it's enough to drive the man inside crazy with grief—
outside, with all its machinery and all its art,
a plains night comes down red on treeless space.

Again today, night will fall in no time.
A light will circle the lame, skinny horse.
And the treeless space, in this hopeless landscape
stretched out before me like the body of a hard man,
will suddenly be filled with stars.
We'll reach the inevitable end once more,
which is to say the stage is set
again today for an elaborate nostalgia.
Me,
the man inside,
once more I'll exhibit my customary talent,
and singing an old-fashioned lament
in the reedy voice of my childhood,
once more, by God, it will crush my unhappy heart
to hear you inside my head,

so far
away, as if I were watching you
                        in a smoky, broken mirror...

2
It's spring outside, my dear wife, spring.
Outside on the plain, suddenly the smell
of fresh earth, birds singing, etc.
It's spring, my dear wife,
the plain outside sparkles...
And inside the bed comes alive with bugs,
                        the water jug no longer freezes,
and in the morning sun floods the concrete...
The sun—
every day till noon now
it comes and goes
from me, flashing off
                        and on...
And as the day turns to afternoon, shadows climb the walls,
the glass of the barred window catches fire,
                        and it's night outside,
                        a cloudless spring night...
And inside this is spring's darkest hour.
In short, the demon called freedom,
with its glittering scales and fiery eyes,
possesses the man inside
                        especially in spring...
I know this from experience, my dear wife,
                        from experience...

3
Sunday today.
Today they took me out in the sun for the first time.
And I just stood there, struck for the first time in my life
                    by how far away the sky is,
                    how blue
                    and how wide.
Then I respectfully sat down on the earth.
I leaned back against the wall.
For a moment no trap to fall into,
no struggle, no freedom, no wife.
Only earth, sun, and me...
I am happy.

1938

ON DEATH AGAIN

My wife,
        life of my life,
                my Pirayé,
I'm thinking about death,
which means my arteries
                are hardening...
One day
        when it's snowing,
or one night
or
    in the heat of one noon,
which of us will die first,
how
        and where?
How
        and what will be
the last sound the one dying hears,
                the last color seen,
the first movement of the one left behind,
                the first words,
                the first food tasted?
Maybe we will die far apart.
The news
        will come screaming,
or someone will just hint at it
and go away, leaving alone
                the one left behind...
And the one left behind
        will be lost in the crowd.
I mean, that's life...
And all these possibilities,
                what year in the 1900's,
                which month,

                which day,
                what hour?

My wife,
        life of my life,
                my Pirayé,
I'm thinking about death,
about our life passing.
I'm sad,
        at peace,
                and proud.
Whoever dies first,
however
and wherever we die,
you and I
        can say we loved
each other
and the people's greatest cause
                —we fought for it—
we can say
        "We lived."

1939

ISTANBUL HOUSE OF DETENTION

In the Istanbul Detention House yard
on a sunny winter day after rain,
as clouds, red tiles, walls, and my face
               trembled in puddles on the ground,
I—with what was bravest and meanest in me,
what was strongest and weakest—
I thought of the world, my country, and you.

1
My love,
they're on the march:
heads forward, eyes wide open,
the red glare of burning cities,
                     crops trampled,
                     endless
                             footsteps.
And people slaughtered:
               like trees and calves,
               only easier
                     and faster.

My love,
amid these footsteps and this slaughter
I sometimes lost my freedom, bread, and you,
but never my faith in the days that will come
out of the darkness, screams, and hunger
to knock on our door with hands full of sun.

2
I'm wonderfully happy I came into the world:
I love its earth, light, struggle, bread.

Although I know its dimensions from pole to pole
                              to the centimeter,
and while I'm not unaware it's a mere toy next to the sun,
the world for me is unbelievably big.
I would have liked to go around the world
and see the fish, fruits, and stars I haven't seen.
However,
I made my European trip only in books and pictures.
In my whole life I never got one letter
                    with its blue stamp canceled in Asia.
Me and our corner grocer,
we're both mightily unknown in America.
Nevertheless,
from China to Spain, from the Cape of Good Hope to Alaska,
in every nautical mile, in every kilometer, I have friends
                                    and enemies.
Such friends that we haven't met even once
yet we can die for the same bread, the same freedom, the same
    dream.
And such enemies that they thirst for my blood—
                    I thirst for theirs.
My strength
is that I'm not alone in this big world.
The world and its people are no secret in my heart,
                    no mystery in my science.
Calmly and openly
          I took my place
                    in the great struggle.
And without it,
          you and the earth
                    are not enough for me.
And yet you are astonishingly beautiful,
                    the earth is warm and beautiful.

3

I love my country:
I've taken the girth of its plane trees in my arms,
I've slept in its prisons.
Nothing lifts my spirits like its songs and tobacco.

My country:
Bedreddin, Sinan, Yunus Emré, and Sakarya,
lead domes and factory chimneys—
it's all the work of my people, whose drooping mustaches
hide their smiles
even from themselves.

My country:
so big
it seems endless.
Edirné, Izmir, Ulukishla, Marash, Trabzon, Erzurum.
All I know of the Erzurum plateau are its songs,
and I'm ashamed to say
I never crossed the Tauruses
to visit the cotton pickers
                                in the south.

My country:
camels, trains, Fords, and sick donkeys,
poplars,
            willow trees,
                            and red earth.

My country:
goats on the Ankara plain,
the sheen of their long blond silky hair.
The succulent plump hazelnuts of Giresun.
Amasya apples with fragrant red cheeks,

olives,
        figs,
                melons,
and bunches and bunches of grapes
                                all colors,
then plows
and black oxen,
and then my people,
        ready to embrace
                with the wide-eyed joy of children
anything modern, beautiful, and good—
my honest, hard-working, brave people,
        half full, half hungry,
                        half slaves. . .

February 1939

HELLO

Nazim, what happiness
that, open and confident,
you can say "Hello"
from the bottom of your heart!

The year is 1940.
The month, July.
The day is the first Thursday of the month.
The hour: 9.

Date your letters in detail this way.
We live in such a world
                that the month, day, and hour
                speak volumes.

Hello, everybody.

To say a big
                fat "Hello"
and then, without finishing my sentence,
                to look at you with a smile
—sly and gleeful—
                            and wink...

We're such perfect friends
                that we understand each other
                            without words or writing...

Hello, everybody,
hello to all of you...

LETTERS FROM CHANKIRI PRISON

1
Four o'clock,
            no you.
Five o'clock,
            nothing.
Six, seven,
tomorrow,
the day after,
and maybe—
            who knows...

I had a garden
      in the prison yard.
About fifteen paces long,
      at the foot of a sunny wall.
You used to come,
and we'd sit side by side,
your big red
      oilcloth bag
                  on your knees...

Remember "Head" Mehmet?
From the juveniles ward.
Square head,
thick short legs,
and hands bigger than his feet.
With a rock he'd brained a guy
      whose hive he robbed of honey.
He used to call you "Good lady."
He had a garden smaller than mine
                  right above me,
                        nearer the sun,
                  in a tin can.

Do you remember a Saturday,
a late afternoon sprinkled
                    by the prison fountain?
The tinsmith Shaban sang a song,
remember:
          "Beypazari is my home, my city—
          who knows where I'll leave my body?"

I did so many pictures of you,
and you didn't leave me even one.
All I have is a photograph:
in another garden,
                    very at ease,
                    very happy,
          you're feeding some chickens
                    and laughing.

The prison garden didn't have any chickens,
but we could laugh all right
                    and we weren't unhappy.
How we heard news
                    of beautiful freedom,
how we listened for the footsteps
                    of good news coming,
what beautiful things we talked about
                    in the prison garden...

2
One afternoon
we sat
at the prison gate
and read Ghazali's rubaiyat:
"Night:
          the great azure garden.

The gold-spangled whirling of the dancers.
And the dead stretched out in their wooden boxes."

If one day,
far from me,
life weighs on you
like a dark rain,
　　　read Ghazali again.
And I know,
my Pirayé,
you'll feel only pity
for his desperate loneliness
　　　　　and awful dread
　　　　　of death.

Let flowing water bring Ghazali to you:
"The king is but an earthen bowl
　　　on the Potter's shelf,
and victories are told
　　　on the ruined walls of the king of kings."

Welling up and springing forth.
Cold
　　　hot
　　　　　cool.
And in the great azure garden,
　　　　　　　the eternal
　　　　　　　ceaseless turning
　　　　　　　of the dancers.

I don't know why
I keep thinking
of a Chankiri saying
I first heard from you:

"When the poplars are in bloom,
                     cherries will come soon."
The poplars are blooming in Ghazali,
but
the master doesn't see
                     the cherries coming.
That's why he worships death.

Upstairs, "Sugar" Ali plays his music.
Evening.
Outside, everybody's shouting.
Water is flowing from the fountain.
And in the light of the guardhouse,
tied to the acacias, three baby wolves.
Beyond the bars
        my great azure garden opens up.
W h a t   i s   r e a l   i s   l i f e . . .

Don't forget me, Piraye. . .

3
Wednesday today—
you know,
Chankiri's market day.
Its eggs and bulgur,
its gilded purple eggplants,
will even reach us,
passing through our iron door in reed baskets. . .

Yesterday
I watched them come down from the villages
tired,
wily,
        and suspicious,

with sorrow under their brows.
They passed by—the men on donkeys,
the women on bare feet.
You probably know some of them.
And the last two Wednesdays they probably missed
          the red-scarfed, "not-uppity"
          lady from Istanbul...

20 July 1940

4
The heat is like nothing you've ever known,
and I who grew up by the sea—
the sea is so far away...

Between two and five
I lie under the mosquito net
—soaking wet,
motionless,
eyes open—
and listen to the flies buzz.
I know
in the yard now
they're splashing water on the walls,
steam rising from the hot red stones.
And outside, skirting the burnt grass
of the fortress, the black-
bricked city stands
in nitric acid light...

Nights a wind comes up suddenly
and suddenly dies.
And the heat, panting like a beast
in the dark, moves on soft furry feet,

threatening me with something.
And from time to time
I shiver in my skin,
                    afraid of nature...

There may be an earthquake.
It's just three days away.
The danger rocked Yozgat.
And the people here say:
because it sits on a salt mine,
            Chankiri will collapse
                    forty days before doomsday.
To go to bed one night
and not wake up in the morning,
                your head smashed by a wooden beam.
What a blind, good-for-nothing death.
I want to live a little longer,
a good deal longer.
I want this for many things,
for many
very important things.

                                        12 August 1940

5
It gets dark at five
with clouds on the attack.
They clearly carry rain.
Many
pass low enough to touch.
The hundred watts in my room
and the tailors' oil lamps are lit.
The tailors are drinking linden tea...
Which means winter's here...

I'm cold.
But not sad.
This privilege is reserved for us:
on winter days in prison,
and not just in prison
but in the big world
        that should
            and will
                be warm,
                    to be cold
                    but not sad. . .

26 October 1940

A STRANGE FEELING

"The plum trees
         are in bloom
—the wild apricot flowers first,
                the plum last. . .

My love,
let's sit
knee to knee
on the grass.
The air is delicious and light
—but not really warm yet—
and the almonds are green
             and fuzzy, still
                 very soft. . .

We're happy
         because we're alive.
We'd probably have been killed long ago
if you were in London,
if I were in Tobruk or on an English freighter. . .

Put your hands on your knees, my love
—your wrists thick and white—
and open your left hand:
the daylight is inside your palm
            like an apricot. . .
Of the people dead in yesterday's air raid,
         about a hundred were under five,
twenty-four still babies. . .

I like the color of pomegranate seeds, my love
—a pomegranate seed, seed of light—
I like melons fragrant,
my plums tart. . ."

... a rainy day
far from fruits and you
—not a single tree has bloomed yet,
and there's even a chance of snow—
in Bursa Prison,
carried away by a strange feeling
and about to explode,
I write this out of pigheadedness
—out of sheer spite—for myself and the people I love.

7 February 1941

LETTER FROM MY WIFE

I
want to die before you.
Do you think the one who follows
finds the one who went first?
I don't think so.
It would be best to have me burned
and put in a jar
              over your fireplace.
Make the jar
clear glass,
              so you can watch me inside...
You see my sacrifice:
I give up being earth,
I give up being a flower,
                        just to stay near you.
And I become dust
to live with you.
Then, when you die,
you can come into my jar
and we'll live there together,
your ashes with mine,
until some dizzy bride
or wayward grandson
tosses us out...
But
by then
we'll be
so mixed
together
that even at the dump our atoms
                    will fall side by side.
We'll dive into the earth together.
And if one day a wild flower

finds water and springs up from that piece of earth,
its stem will have
two blooms for sure:
                        one will be you,
                        the other me.

I'm
not about to die yet.
I want to bear another child.
I'm brimming with life.
My blood is hot.
I'm going to live a long, long time—
and with you.
Death doesn't scare me,
I just don't find our funeral arrangements
                        too attractive.
But everything could change
before I die.
Any chance you'll get out of prison soon?
Something inside me says:
                        Maybe.

                                    18 February 1945

9-10 P.M. POEMS

How beautiful to think of you:
amid news of death and victory,
in prison,
when I'm past forty...

How beautiful to think of you:
your hand resting on blue cloth,
your hair grave and soft
like my beloved Istanbul earth...
The joy of loving you
       is like a second person inside me...
The smell of geranium leaves on my fingers,
a sunny quiet,
and the call of flesh:
     a warm
           deep darkness
                  parted by bright red lines...

How beautiful to think of you,
to write about you,
to sit back in prison and remember you:
what you said on this or that day in such and such a place,
                    not the words themselves
                    but the world in their aura...

How beautiful to think of you.
I must carve you something from wood—
                  a box,
                        a ring—
and weave you about three meters of fine silk.
And jumping
     right up
and grabbing the iron bars at my window,

I must shout out the things I write for you
                        to the milk-white blue of freedom. . .

How beautiful to think of you:
amid news of death and victory,
in prison,
when I'm past forty. . .

20 September 1945

At this late hour
this fall night
            I am full of your words:
words
        eternal like time and matter,
                naked like eyes,
                        heavy like hands,
        and bright like stars.

Your words came
from your heart, flesh, and mind.
They brought you:
                    mother,
                        wife,
                            and friend.
They were sad, painful, happy, hopeful, brave—
                    your words were *human*. . .

21 September 1945

Our son is sick,
his father's in prison,
your head is heavy in your tired hands:
our fate is like the world's. . .

People bring better days,
our son gets well,
his father comes out of prison,
your gold eyes smile:
our fate is like the world's...

22 September 1945

I read a book,
            you are in it;
I hear a song,
            you're in it.
I eat my bread,
                you're sitting facing me;
I work,
        and you sit watching me.
You who are everywhere my "Ever Present,"
                        I cannot talk with you,
                        we cannot hear each other's voice:
you are my eight-year widow...

23 September 1945

What is she doing now,
            right now, this instant?
Is she in the house or outside?
Is she working, lying down, or standing up?
Maybe she's just raised her arm—
hey,
        how this suddenly bares her thick white wrist!

What is she doing now,
            right now, this instant?

Maybe she's petting
                    a kitten on her lap.
Or maybe she's walking, about to take a step—
those beloved feet that take her straight to me
                              on my dark days!
And what's she thinking about—
                              me?
Or—
      oh, I don't know—
                          why the beans refuse to cook?
Or else
          why most people are this unhappy?

What is she doing now,
              right now, this instant?

24 September 1945

The most beautiful sea
                    hasn't been crossed yet.
The most beautiful child
                    hasn't grown up yet.
Our most beautiful days
                    we haven't seen yet.
And the most beautiful words I wanted to tell you
                    I haven't said yet...

25 September 1945

Nine o'clock.
The bell struck in the town square,
the ward doors will close any minute.
Prison has lasted a bit long this time:
                          eight years...

Living is a matter of hope, my love.
Living
       is a serious business, like loving you. . .

26 September 1945

They've taken us prisoner,
they've locked us up:
              me inside the walls,
                   you outside.
But that's nothing.
The worst
is when people—knowingly or not—
carry prison inside themselves. . .
Most people have been forced to do this,
honest, hard-working, good people
who deserve to be loved as much as I love you. . .

30 September 1945

Thinking of you is beautiful
                  and hopeful,
like listening to the best voice in the world
           sing the loveliest song.
But hope is not enough for me:
I no longer want to listen,
               I want to sing the songs. . .

1 October 1945

Over the mountain:
a cloud flush with evening sun over the mountain.

Today, too:
today, too, passed without you—I mean, without half the world.
Soon they'll open
red on red:
soon the four-o'clocks will open red on red.
In the air, brave soundless wings bridge
          our separation, which feels like exile...

2 October 1945

The wind blows on, the same cherry branch
doesn't bend in the same wind even once.
Birds chirp in the tree:
                              the wings want to fly.
The door is closed:
                              it wants to break open.
I want you:
life should be
beautiful like you,
          friendly and loving...
I know the feast of poverty
                              still isn't over...
It will be yet...

5 October 1945

We both know, my love,
they taught us:
     how to be hungry, cold,
     tired to death,
     and apart.
We haven't been forced to kill yet
or to go through the business of being killed.

We both know, my love,
we can teach:
     how to fight for our people
     and how—a little better
          and deeper each day—
               to love...

6 October 1945

Clouds pass, heavy with news.
The letter that didn't come crumples in my hand.
My heart is at the tips of my eyelashes,
     blessing the earth that disappears into the distance.
I want to call out: "P i r a y é ,
          P i r a y é !"

7 October 1945

At night human cries
             cross the open sea
                  with the winds.
It's not safe yet
        to sail the open sea at night...

The fields haven't been plowed for six years—
tank treads still track the earth.
Snow
     will bury the tank tracks this winter.

Ah, light of my life,
the antennas are lying again
so the merchants of sweat can close their books
          with a hundred-percent profit.

But those back from feasting at Azrael's table
                    have come back with sealed fates...

8 October 1945

    I've become impossible again:
                    sleepless, irritable, perverse.
One day
        I work
as if beating a wild beast, as if cursing all that's holy,
    and the next day
I lie on my back from morning to night,
    a lazy song on my lips like an unlit cigarette.
And it drives me crazy,
                    the hatred
                            and pity I feel for myself...

    I've become impossible again:
                    sleepless, irritable, perverse.
Again, as always, I'm wrong.
I have no cause
                    and couldn't possibly.
What I'm doing is shameful,
                            a disgrace.
But I can't help it:
                    I'm jealous of you,
                    forgive me...

9 October 1945

Last night I saw you in a dream:
sitting at my knee, you raised your head
and looked at me with your big gold eyes.

You were asking something.
Your moist lips opened and closed,
                    but I couldn't hear your voice.

Somewhere in the night a clock struck like good news.
The air whispered of infinity.
I heard "Memo"—my canary—singing in his red cage,
the crackle of seeds pushing through a plowed field,
and the righteous, triumphant hum of a crowd.
Your moist lips still opened and closed,
                    but I couldn't hear your voice. . .

I woke up broken.
I had fallen asleep over a book.
I thought:
            Were all those sounds your voice?

10 October 1945

When I gaze into your eyes
            the smell of sunny earth hits me:
            I'm in a wheatfield, lost amid the grain.

The bottomless green-glittering abyss
of your eyes is ever-changing like eternal matter,
            which forever gives away its secrets
            but will never
            wholly surrender. . .

18 October 1945

As I go out the castle door to meet my death,
my love, I can say

to the city I see for the last time:
    "Although you didn't make me all that happy,
    I did my best
            to make you
                    happy.
    You continue on your way to happiness,
                        life continues.
    I'm at peace,
    my heart satisfied with earning your bread,
    my eyes sad to be leaving your light.
                    I came and here I go—
                    be of good cheer, Aleppo..."

27 October 1945

We are one half of an apple,
            the other half is this big world.
We are one half of an apple,
            the other half is our people.
You are one half of an apple,
            the other half is me,
                    us two...

28 October 1945

The swelling fragrance of the rose geranium,
the humming of the sea,
and fall is here with its full clouds and wise earth...

My love,
the years have ripened.
We've gone through so much
    we could be a thousand years old.

But we are still
     wide-eyed children
          running barefoot in the sun, hand in hand. . .

5 November 1945

Forget the flowering almonds.
They aren't worth it:
in this business
     what cannot come back should not be remembered.
Dry your hair in the sun:
     let the wet, heavy reds
          glow with the languor of ripe fruit. . .
My love, my love,
     the season
          fall. . .

8 November 1945

Over the rooftops of my far-off city
under the Sea of Marmara
and across the fall earth
          your voice came
             rich and liquid.
For three minutes.
Then the phone went black. . .

12 November 1945

The last south winds blow warm,
     humming like blood spurting from an artery.
I listen to the air:
     the pulse has slowed.

There's snow on Mount Uludagh,
and on Cherry Hill the bears have gone to sleep
                    on red chestnut leaves, cuddly and grand.
The poplars are undressing on the plain.
The silkworm eggs are moved inside for the winter,
fall is almost over,
the earth is sinking into its pregnant sleep.
And we will pass another winter
                    in our great anger,
                         warmed by the fire of our sacred hope...

13 November 1945

The poverty of Istanbul—they say—defies description,
hunger—they say—has ravaged the people,
TB—they say—is everywhere.
Little girls this high—they say—
                    in burned-out buildings, movie theaters...

Dark news comes from my far-off city
of honest, hard-working, poor people—
                              the real Istanbul,
which is your home, my love,
and which I carry in the bag on my back
        wherever I'm exiled, to whatever prison,
             the city I hold in my heart like the loss of a child,
             like your image in my eyes...

20 November 1945

Though an occasional carnation still blooms in the flowerpots,
the fall plowing is over on the plain:
                    they're sowing seeds now.

And picking olives.
Both moving into winter
and making way for the spring shoots.
And me, full of you
       and loaded with the impatience of great journeys,
       I lie in Bursa like an anchored freighter. . .

4 December 1945

Take out the dress I first saw you in,
look your best,
look like spring trees. . .
Wear in your hair
       the carnation I sent you in a letter from prison,
raise your kissable, lined, broad white forehead.
Today, not broken and sad—
                no way!—
today Nazim Hikmet's woman must be beautiful
          like a rebel flag. . .

5 December 1945

The keel has snapped,
the slaves are breaking their chains.
That's a northeaster blowing,
it'll smash the hull on the rocks.
This world, this pirate ship, will sink—
          come hell or high water, it will sink.
And we will build a world as hopeful, free,
          and open as your forehead, my Piraye. . .

6 December 1945

They are the enemies of hope, my love,
of flowing water
            and the fertile tree,
            of life growing and unfolding.
Death has branded them—
                  rotting teeth, decaying flesh—
            and soon they will be dead and gone for good.
And yes, my love,
freedom will walk around swinging its arms
in its Sunday best—workers' overalls!—
                  yes, freedom in this beautiful country. . .

7 December 1945

They're the enemy of Rejeb, the towel man in Bursa,
of the fitter Hassan in the Karabuk factory,
of the poor peasant woman Hatijé,
of the day laborer Suleiman,
they're your enemy and mine,
the enemy of anyone who thinks,
and this country, the home of these people—
my love, they're the enemy of this country. . .

12 December 1945

The trees on the plain make one last effort to shine:
                  spangled gold
                        copper
                              bronze and wood. . .
The feet of the oxen sink softly into the moist earth.

And the mountains are plunged in fog:
                    lead-gray, soaking wet...
That's it—
fall must be finally over today.
Wild geese just shot by,
                    probably headed for Iznik Lake.
The air is cool
        and smells something like soot:
        the smell of snow is in the air.

To be outside now,
        to ride a horse at full gallop toward the mountains...
You'll say, "You don't know how to ride a horse,"
but don't laugh
            or get jealous:
I've picked up a new habit in prison,
I love nature nearly as much
                    as I love you.
                    And both of you are far away...

13 December 1945

Snow came on suddenly at night.
Morning was crows exploding from white branches.
Winter on the Bursa plain as far as the eye can see:
a world without end.
My love,
the season's changed
            in one leap after great labor.
And under the snow, proud
                    hard-working life
                            continues...

14 December 1945

Damn it, winter has come down hard...
You and my honest Istanbul, who knows how you are?
Do you have coal?
Could you buy wood?
Line the windows with newspaper.
Go to bed early.
Probably nothing's left in the house to sell.
To be cold and half hungry:
              here, too, we're the majority
              in the world, our country, and our city...

ONE NIGHT OF KNEE-DEEP SNOW

One night of knee-deep snow
my adventure started—
pulled from the supper table,
thrown into a police car,
packed off on a train,
and locked up in a room.
Its ninth year ended three days ago.

In the corridor a man on a stretcher
is dying open-mouthed on his back,
the grief of long iron years in his face.

I think of isolation,
            sickening and total,
                        like that of the mad and the dead:
first, seventy-six days
        of a closed door's silent hostility,
then seven weeks in a ship's hold.
Still, I wasn't defeated:
my head
            was a second person at my side.

I've forgotten most of their faces
—all I remember is a very long pointed nose—
yet how many times they lined up before me!
When my sentence was read, they had one worry:
                                    to look imposing.
                                    They did not.
They looked more like things than people:
like wall clocks, stupid
                    and arrogant,
and sad and pitiful like handcuffs, chains, etc.

A city without houses or streets.
Tons of hope, tons of grief.
The distances microscopic.
Of the four-legged creatures, just cats.

I live in a world of forbidden things!
To smell your lover's cheek:
                                forbidden.
To eat at the same table with your children:
                                                forbidden.
To talk with your brother or your mother
    without a wire screen or a guard between you:
                                                forbidden.
To seal a letter you've written
or to get a letter still sealed:
                                forbidden.
To turn off the light when you go to bed:
                                        forbidden.
To play backgammon:
                        forbidden.
And not that it isn't forbidden,
    but what you can hide in your heart and have in your hand
        is to love, think, and understand.

In the corridor the man on the stretcher died.
They took him away.
Now no hope, no grief,
                no bread, no water,
                no freedom, no prison,
                no wanting women, no guards, no bedbugs,
                and no more cats to sit and stare at him.
                        That business is finished, over.

But mine goes on:
my head keeps loving, thinking, understanding,
my impotent rage goes on eating me,
and, since morning, my liver goes on aching...

1946

HAZEL ARE MY LADY'S EYES

Hazel are my lady's eyes,
with waves and waves of green:
gold leaf overlaid with green moiré.
Brothers, what's the story?
For nine years our hands haven't touched—
I got old here,
she there.

My girl, your thick white neck is lined,
but we can't possibly get old
—we need another word for sagging flesh—
because you're old
only if you love no one but yourself.

1947

SINCE I WAS THROWN INSIDE

Since I was thrown inside
     the earth has gone around the sun ten times.
If you ask it:
         "Not worth mentioning—
            a microscopic span."
If you ask me:
         "Ten years of my life."
I had a pencil
     the year I was thrown inside.
I used it up after a week of writing.
If you ask it:
         "A whole lifetime."
If you ask me:
         "What's a week."

Since I've been inside
     Osman did his seven-and-a-half
         for manslaughter and left,
         knocked around on the outside for a while,
         then landed back inside for smuggling,
         served six months, and got out again;
         yesterday we had a letter—he's married,
         with a kid coming in the spring.

They're ten years old now
     the children who were born
         the year I was thrown inside.
And that year's foals, shaky on their spindly long legs,
     have been wide-rumped, contented mares for some time.
But the olive seedlings are still saplings,
               still children.

New squares have opened in my far-off city
                                     since I was thrown inside.
And my family now lives
      in a house I haven't seen
            on a street I don't know.

Bread was like cotton, soft and white,
                                 the year I was thrown inside.
Then it was rationed,
and here inside men killed each other
                over black loaves the size of fists.
Now it's free again
but dark and tasteless.

The year I was thrown inside
        the SECOND hadn't started yet.

The ovens at Dachau hadn't been lit,
nor the atom bomb dropped on Hiroshima.

Time flowed like blood from a child's slit throat.
Then that chapter was officially closed.
Now the American dollar talks of a THIRD.

Still, the day has gotten lighter
                  since I was thrown inside.
And "at the edge of darkness,
      pushing against the earth with their heavy hands,
            THEY've risen up" halfway.

Since I was thrown inside
      the earth has gone around the sun ten times.
And I repeat once more with the same passion
      what I wrote about THEM
           the year I was thrown inside:

"They who are numberless like ants in the earth,
                          fish in the sea,
                                    birds in the air,
who are cowardly, brave,
                    ignorant, wise,
                              and childlike,
and who destroy
        and create,
my songs tell only of their adventures."
                          And anything else,
                                    such as my ten years here,
                                          is just so much talk.

1947

THE STRANGEST CREATURE ON EARTH

You're like a scorpion, my brother,
you live in cowardly darkness
                    like a scorpion.
You're like a sparrow, my brother,
always in a sparrow's flutter.
You're like a clam, my brother,
closed like a clam, content.
And you're frightening, my brother,
                    like the mouth of an extinct volcano.

Not one,
       not five—
unfortunately, you number millions.
You're like a sheep, my brother:
                when the cloaked drover raises his stick,
                    you quickly join the flock
and run, almost proudly, to the slaughterhouse.
I mean, you're the strangest creature on earth—
even stranger than the fish
               that couldn't see the ocean for the water.
And the oppression in this world
                 is thanks to you.
And if we're hungry, tired, covered with blood,
and still being crushed like grapes for our wine,
                   the fault is yours—
I can hardly bring myself to say it,
but most of the fault, my dear brother, is yours.

1947

ON IBRAHIM BALABAN'S "SPRING PAINTING"

Here, eyes, see Balaban's art.
Here is dawn: the month is May.
Here is light:
        smart, brave, fresh, alive, pitiless.
Here are clouds:
         like whipped cream.
Here, mountains:
         cool and blue.
Here are foxes on their morning rounds—
light on their long tails,
    alarm on their pointed noses.
Here, eyes, look:
hungry, hairs raised, red-mouthed,
here on a mountaintop, a wolf.
Haven't you ever felt
the rage of a hungry wolf at sunrise?
Here, eyes, see: butterflies, bees,
the flash of sparkling fish.
Here, a stork
        just back from Egypt.
Here is a deer,
        creature of a more beautiful world.
Here, eyes, see the bear outside its den,
         still sleepy.
Haven't you ever thought of living
unconsciously like bears, sniffing the earth,
close to pears and the mossy dark,
far from human voices and fire?
Here, eyes, look: squirrels, rabbits,
lizards, turtles,
our grape-eyed donkey.
Here, eyes, see
a shimmering tree,

most like a person in its beauty.
Here is green grass:

          go ahead, my bare feet.
Here, nose, smell:

          mint, thyme.
Here, mouth, water:

          sorrels, mallows.
Touch, hands, caress, hold—
here, my mother's milk,

    my wife's flesh,

        my child's smile.
Here is plowed earth,
here is man:
lord of rocks and mountains, the birds and the beasts.
Here are his sandals, here the patches on his breeches.
Here is the plow,
and here are the oxen with sad, terrible sores on their rumps.

1947

ABOUT MOUNT ULUDAGH

For seven years now Uludagh and I
    have stared each other in the eye.
It hasn't budged an inch
    and neither have I,
yet we know each other well.
Like anything living, it can laugh and get mad.

Sometimes
    in winter, especially at night,
        when the wind blows from the south,
with its snowy pine forests, plateaus, and frozen lakes
        it rolls over in its sleep,
and the Old Man who lives way at the top
        —long beard flying,
                skirts billowing—
rides the howling wind down into the valley...

Then sometimes,
    especially in May, at sunup,
    it rises like a brand-new world—
        huge, blue, vast,
        free and happy.

Then there are days
    it looks like its picture on the pop bottles.
And in its hotel I can't see, I know
        lady skiers sipping cognac
        are flirting with the gentleman skiers.

And the day arrives
when one of its beetle-browed mountain folk, having
butchered his neighbor at the altar of sacred property,
    comes to us like a guest in his yellow homespun trousers
        to do fifteen years in Cell Block 71.

1947

ON LIVING

I

Living is no laughing matter:
        you must live with great seriousness
                like a squirrel, for example—
    I mean without looking for something beyond and above living,
                I mean living must be your whole occupation.
Living is no laughing matter:
        you must take it seriously,
        so much so and to such a degree
    that, for example, your hands tied behind your back,
                        your back to the wall,
    or else in a laboratory
        in your white coat and safety glasses,
        you can die for people—
even for people whose faces you've never seen,
even though you know living
        is the most real, the most beautiful thing.
I mean, you must take living so seriously
    that even at seventy, for example, you'll plant olive trees—
    and not for your children, either,
    but because although you fear death you don't believe it,
    because living, I mean, weighs heavier.

II

Let's say we're seriously ill, need surgery—
which is to say we might not get up
                from the white table.
Even though it's impossible not to feel sad
                about going a little too soon,
we'll still laugh at the jokes being told,

we'll look out the window to see if it's raining,
or still wait anxiously
                    for the latest newscast...
Let's say we're at the front—
                    for something worth fighting for, say.
There, in the first offensive, on that very day,
            we might fall on our face, dead.
We'll know this with a curious anger,
            but we'll still worry ourselves to death
            about the outcome of the war, which could last years.
Let's say we're in prison
and close to fifty,
and we have eighteen more years, say,
                    before the iron doors will open.
We'll still live with the outside,
with its people and animals, struggle and wind—
                    I mean with the outside beyond the walls.
I mean, however and wherever we are,
            we must live as if we will never die.

III

This earth will grow cold,
a star among stars
                and one of the smallest,
a gilded mote on blue velvet—
            I mean *this*, our great earth.
This earth will grow cold one day,
not like a block of ice
or a dead cloud even
but like an empty walnut it will roll along
                in pitch-black space...

You must grieve for this right now
—you have to feel this sorrow now—
for the world must be loved this much
             if you're going to say "I lived"...

February 1948

IT'S THIS WAY

I stand in the advancing light,
my hands hungry, the world beautiful.

My eyes can't get enough of the trees—
they're so hopeful, so green.

A sunny road runs through the mulberries,
I'm at the window of the prison infirmary.

I can't smell the medicines—
carnations must be blooming nearby.

It's this way:
being captured is beside the point,
the point is not to surrender.

1948

ANGINA PECTORIS

If half my heart is here, doctor,
    the other half is in China
with the army flowing
    toward the Yellow River.
And every morning, doctor,
every morning at sunrise my heart
    is shot in Greece.
And every night, doctor,
when the prisoners are asleep and the infirmary is deserted,
my heart stops at a run-down old house
                    in Istanbul.

And then after ten years
all I have to offer my poor people
is this apple in my hand, doctor,
one red apple:
        my heart.
And that, doctor, that is the reason
for this angina pectoris—
not nicotine, prison, or arteriosclerosis.
I look at the night through the bars,
and despite the weight on my chest
my heart still beats with the most distant stars.

April 1948

ALAMEDA FREE LIBRARY

I MADE A JOURNEY

Far off in the night,
    airport lights burned into the sky
like white fire,
and the trains I missed dived sparkling into the darkness,
    taking part of me away.
I made a journey.

I made a journey.
People's eyes were all white,
the putrid waters stank.
I passed through the swamp of lies and stupidity
    without getting lost in the head-high reeds. . .

I made a journey
with women sitting doubled over,
    their fists pressed to their flat bellies,
or running barefooted before the wind;
with the dead;
with those forgotten on battlefields and barricades.

I made a journey,
riding on trucks
    carrying prisoners
        through cities,
            the asphalt moist in the morning light. . .

I made a journey—
I couldn't get my fill of the grapes crushed by your white teeth
or of your bed like a shuttered summer afternoon.

I made a journey:
brand-new buildings waited in warehouses,
hope shone bright green like a young pine,

and lamps blazed on foreheads
    a thousand meters underground.

I made a journey
under the moon,
in the light of the sun and rain,
with the four seasons and all time,
with insects, grass, and stars,
and with the earth's honest people—
I mean, affectionate as a violin,
pitiless and brave
as a child who can't speak yet,
ready to die with the ease of a bird
    or live a thousand years. . .

1948

OCCUPATION

As dawn breaks on the horns of my ox,
I plow the earth with patient pride.
The earth is moist and warm on my bare feet.

I beat iron all morning—
the darkness is dyed red.

In the afternoon heat I pick olives,
the leaves the loveliest of greens:
I'm light from head to toe.

Guests come without fail each evening,
my door is wide open
                              to all songs.

At night I wade knee-deep into the water
and pull the nets out of the sea:
the fish get all mixed up with the stars.

Now I'm responsible
                              for the state of the world:
people and earth, darkness and light.

So you see I'm up to my ears in work.
Don't bother me with talk, my rose,
I'm busy falling in love with you.

1948

SADNESS

Is the sadness I feel
    these sunny winter days
    the longing to be somewhere else—
    on the bridge in my Istanbul, say,
    or with the workers in Adana
    or in the Greek mountains or in China,
    or beside her who no longer loves me?

Or is it a trick
             of my liver,
has a dream put me in this state,
or is it loneliness again
or the fact
         I'm pushing fifty?

The second chapter
of my sadness
    will tiptoe out
         and go the way it came—
    if I can just finish this poem
    or sleep a little better,
    if I just get a letter
    or some good news on the radio. . .

1949

SOME ADVICE TO THOSE WHO WILL SERVE TIME IN PRISON

If instead of being hanged by the neck
   you're thrown inside
   for not giving up hope
in the world, your country, and people,
   if you do ten or fifteen years
   apart from the time you have left,
you won't say,
     "Better I had swung from the end of a rope
        like a flag"—
you'll put your foot down and live.
It may not be a pleasure exactly,
but it's your solemn duty
   to live one more day
     to spite the enemy.
Part of you may live alone inside,
   like a stone at the bottom of a well.
But the other part
   must be so caught up
   in the flurry of the world
   that you shiver there inside
  when outside, at forty days' distance, a leaf moves.
To wait for letters inside,
to sing sad songs,
or to lie awake all night staring at the ceiling
    is sweet but dangerous.
Look at your face from shave to shave,
forget your age,
watch out for lice
   and for spring nights,
  and always remember
   to eat every last piece of bread—
also, don't forget to laugh heartily.

And who knows,
the woman you love may stop loving you.
Don't say it's no big thing:
it's like the snapping of a green branch
                            to the man inside.
To think of roses and gardens inside is bad,
to think of seas and mountains is good.
Read and write without rest,
and I also advise weaving
and making mirrors.
I mean, it's not that you can't pass
        ten or fifteen years inside
                        and more—
            you can,
            as long as the jewel
            on the left side of your chest doesn't lose its luster!

May 1949

Late Poems

AWAKENING

You woke up.
Where are you?
At home.
You can't get used
      to waking up
      in your own house.
This is the kind of daze
      thirteen years of prison leaves you in.
Who's sleeping next to you?
It's not loneliness—it's your wife.
She's sleeping peacefully, like an angel.
Pregnancy becomes the lady.
What time is it?
Eight.
You're safe till night.
Because it's the custom:
      the police don't raid houses in broad daylight.

1950

THE EVENING WALK

You no sooner got out of prison
than you made your wife
                    pregnant;
she's on your arm,
            and you're taking an evening walk
                            around the neighborhood.
The lady's belly comes up to her nose.
She carries her sacred charge coyly;
you're respectful and proud.
The air is cool
like baby hands.
You want to hold it in your palms
                    and warm it up.
The neighborhood cats wait at the butcher's door,
and upstairs his curly-haired wife
has settled her breasts on the window sill,
                            watching the evening.
Half-light, spotless sky:
smack in the middle sits the evening star
                    sparkling like a glass of water.
Indian summer lasted long this year—
the mulberry trees are yellow,
                    but the figs are still green.
Refik the typesetter and the milkman Yorgi's middle daughter
            go for an evening stroll,
            their fingers locked.
The grocer Karabet's lights are on.
This Armenian citizen won't forgive
            his father's slaughter in the Kurdish mountains.
But he likes you,
because you also can't forgive
            those who blackened the Turkish people's name.

The tuberculars of the neighborhood and the shut-ins
          peer out from behind glass.
The washwoman Huriyé's unemployed son
                leaves for the coffeehouse
                        with a heavy heart.
Rahmi Bey's radio is giving the news:
in a country in the Far East,
moon-faced yellow people
          are fighting a white dragon.
Of your people,
          four thousand five hundred Mehmets
                  have been sent there to murder their brothers.
You blush
      with rage and shame
and not in general, either—
      this impotent grief
      is all yours.
It's as if they'd knocked your wife down from behind
                        and killed her child,
or you were back in prison
and they were making the peasant guards
                        beat the peasants again.

All of a sudden it's night.
The evening walk is over.
A police jeep turned into your street,
your wife whispered:
                "To our house?"

1950

113

YOU

You are a field,
    I am the tractor.
You are paper,
    I am the typewriter.
My wife, mother of my son,
you are a song—
    I am the guitar.
I'm the warm, humid night the south wind brings—
    you are the woman walking by the water,
        looking across at the lights.
I am water,
    you are the drinker.
I'm the passerby on the road,
    you are the one who opens her window
        and beckons to me.
You are China,
    I am Mao Tse-tung's army.
You're a Filipino girl of fourteen,
    I save you
        from an American sailor's clutches.
You're a mountain village
    in Anatolia,
you're my city,
    most beautiful and most unhappy.
You're a cry for help, I mean you're my country;
    the steps running toward you—that's me.

1951

TO LYDIA IVANNA

How many times we've written poems together,
how many times I've rested my tired head
                    in its smoke-blue hands.
I don't think it will hurt me.
But out of respect for your science
        and to make you happy, Lydia Ivanna,
        okay—I'll give up tobacco,
                    my prison comrade.
Okay, Lydia Ivanna, I won't get drunk:
no wine, no raki, no vodka,
                not even on New Year's Eve
                or holidays
                    or even on Kostya's birthday.
Yes, that's the easiest:
I don't care if I never touch the stuff.
Okay, I'll put my sick heart to bed
at the stroke of ten
with the birds and children.
And yet, late at night
                in winter especially, how I love
to cross Red Square
quietly, without disturbing
                the big man's sleep,
and walk the banks
        of the Moscow River
or, Lydia Ivanna, to sit up till dawn
        in the light of a master's book.
Okay, I'll abstain for at least six months
from my lover's lips.
We're apart anyway.

I know, comrade Lydia Ivanna,
it's imperative I follow your orders—

or else a third coronary,
my heart exploding like a hand grenade.
I know.
But you say joy,
                  anger,
                              and grief
are even worse than tobacco,
worse than no sleep.
Yes, but my dear doctor,
how can I keep from bursting with joy
when, say,
                  I hear we got the most votes
                              in the French elections?
My smart doctor, have a heart:
how can I help getting angry when I think of my country
fighting for its life under the heel of a gang of thugs?
Or look:
                  I may never again see
                  my Memet and his mother—
my bright-eyed doctor,
                              what can I do
                                          but grieve?
In short,
Lydia Ivanna, don't get mad at me
      if your loving labors come to nothing:
I can't promise to be
      calm, dignified,
                  and indifferent,
                  like a rock by the sea...
If my heart's going to break,
                              let it break from anger,
                                          grief,
                                                or joy.

29 April 1953
Moscow, Barviha Hospital

LAST WILL AND TESTAMENT

Comrades, if I don't live to see the day
—I mean, if I die before freedom comes—
take me away
and bury me in a village cemetery in Anatolia.

The worker Osman whom Hassan Bey ordered shot
can lie on one side of me, and on the other side
the martyr Aysha, who gave birth in the rye
and died inside of forty days.

Tractors and songs can pass below the cemetery—
in the dawn light, new people, the smell of burnt gasoline,
fields held in common, water in the canals,
no drought or fear of the police.

Of course, we won't hear those songs:
the dead lie stretched out underground
and rot like black branches,
deaf, dumb, and blind under the earth.

But I sang those songs
before they were written,
I smelled the burnt gasoline
before the blueprints for the tractors were drawn.

As for my neighbors,
the worker Osman and the martyr Aysha,
they felt the great longing while alive,
maybe without even knowing it.

Comrades, if I die before that day, I mean
—and it's looking more and more likely—
bury me in a village cemetery in Anatolia,
and if there's one handy,
             a plane tree could stand at my head,
             I wouldn't need a stone or anything.

1953
Moscow, Barviha Hospital

ABOUT THE SEA

Leaving a jumble of jagged mountains in the west,
our train descended to the warm, humid plain.
A pickup sweated past us on our right,
the driver a dark plump woman in a green dress.
A sailor sat on the burlap sacks in the back,
his cap ribbon flailed in the wind.
A silvery factory with bridges, towers, chimneys, and smoke
passed on our left
like a warship returning to port.

First came its coolness,
and the sharp smell of iodine
mingled with the scent of the apples on the racks.
Then I saw it reflected in the sky:
the air got bluer and bluer.
Then suddenly we were face to face.
It was inside a breakwater,
squeezed between the ships and the docks.
I remembered an eagle at the zoo—
wings drooping at his sides,
sullen head on his chest.

The train entered the station, it disappeared.
The train left the station, again we were suddenly face to face:
the sun rose,
and the cold, steely glare
that studied us through slit-eyes
softened and warmed up at our approach.
I didn't gaze at it and think:
Life bubbles up and dies down like the foam
on this unbounded, endless motion.
I wanted to jump off the car
and run to it, breathless.

Whether in moonlight or broad daylight,
whether it's frothing or flat as a sheet,
to stand on the shore and watch it
kills me.
I feel the sadness
of an empty augur shell.
I must be at the center of its eye—
with fishermen, say, at the nets.
Or, my hand on the tiller,
                    sailing
                            with my lover.
Or at the captain's side in a storm
or swimming against the current.
I must be in the eye of it.

I thought of Engels.
How beautiful to have your ashes scattered at sea!
But me, I want to be put in a pine box
and buried on the Anatolian plateau.
At cherry-blossom time
sailors from many different ships
can come and visit our plateau.
And they can sing the same great song
of many different seas.

1954
Tbilisi-Moscow

ELEGY FOR SATAN

My dog's name was Satan.
"Was" has nothing to do with his name—
nothing happened to his name.
And he wasn't anything like his name.
Devils are cruel:
the cruel are sly and lie,
but they aren't smart.
My dog was smart.

I helped to kill my dog a little, too:
I didn't know how to take care of him.
If you can't care for it,
       don't even plant a tree.
A tree that dries up in your hands
       becomes a curse.
"A person learns to swim in water," you say.
True.
But if you drown,
       you drown alone.

Mornings now I wake up
and listen—
no one scratching at my door.
I feel like crying.
I'm ashamed I can't cry.
He was like a person.
Most animals are like people—
       and like good people, too.
Under the command of friendship, his thick neck was hair-thin.
His freedom was in his teeth and legs,
       his politesse in his long bushy tail.

We used to miss each other.
He would speak of the gravest matters:
of hunger, of being full, of love.
But he didn't know longing for home.
That's on my head.
When the poet went to heaven,
          he said: "Ah, but my country..."

He died
the way everyone dies,
whether human, animal, or plant—
on a bed or on the ground, in the air or in water,
suddenly, waiting, or asleep—
the way everyone dies,
the way I'm going to die,
the way we're going to die...

Today it's ninety-eight in the shade.
I gaze at the forest from the balcony:
tall slender pines rise deep red
against the steel-blue sky.
The people sweating,
the dogs' tongues hanging out,
they're all headed for the lake to swim.
Leaving their heavy bodies on the shore,
they'll know the happiness of fish.

June 1956
Peredelkino

FAUST'S HOUSE

Below the towers, under the arcades,
I wander through Prague late
                              at night.
The sky is an alembic distilling gold in the dark—
an alchemist's still over a deep-blue flame.
I walk down the hill toward Charles Square:
on the corner, next to the clinic there,
            is Doctor Faust's house set back in a garden.

I knock on the door.
The doctor isn't home.
As we all know,
on a night like this
                      about two hundred years ago,
the Devil took him
                    through a hole in the ceiling.

I knock on the door.
In this house I, too, will hand Satan a deed—
I, too, signed the deed with my blood.
I don't want gold from him
              or knowledge or youth.
I've had it with exile,
          I give up!
If I could have just one hour in Istanbul...

I knock and knock on the door.
But the door doesn't open.
Why?
Am I asking the impossible, Mephistopheles?
Or isn't my tattered soul
worth buying?

In Prague the moon is rising lemon-yellow.
I stand outside Doctor Faust's house
at midnight, knocking on the closed door.

22 November 1956

PRAGUE DAWN

In Prague it's growing light
and snowing—
                    sleety,
                              leaden.
In Prague the baroque slowly lights up:
                                        uneasy, distant,
                    its gilt grief-blackened.
The statues on Charles Bridge
        look like birds descended from a dead star.

In Prague the first trolley has left the garage,
its windows glow yellow and warm.
But I know
            it's ice-cold inside:
no passenger's breath has warmed it.
In Prague Pepik drinks his coffee and milk,
the wood table spotless in the white kitchen.
In Prague it's growing light
and snowing—
                    sleety,
                              leaden.

In Prague a cart—
                    a one-horse wagon—
                passes the Old Jewish Cemetery.
The cart is full of longing for another city,
                                I am the driver.
In Prague the baroque slowly lights up:
                                        uneasy, distant,
                    its gilt grief-blackened.
In Prague's Jewish Cemetery, death is breathless, stone-still.
Ah my rose, ah my rose,
exile is worse than death...

20 December 1956

OPTIMISTIC PRAGUE

1957, January 17.
Nine o'clock exactly.
Sun-bright dry cold, no lies,
dry cold rose-pink,
sky-blue dry cold.
My red mustache nearly freezes.
The city of Prague is etched on cut glass
    with a diamond point.
If I touch it, it will ring:
    gold-edged, clear, white.
It's exactly nine o'clock
    on all the towers
        and my watch.
Dry cold sun-bright, rose-pink,
sky-blue dry cold.
It's exactly nine o'clock.
This minute, this second,
    not a single lie was uttered in Prague.
This minute, this second,
    women gave birth without pain,
and not a single hearse
    went down a single street.
This minute
    all the charts climbed
    in favor of the sick.
For a moment
    all the women were beautiful, all the men wise,
    and the manikins weren't sad.
Now
    children answered all the questions in school
    without stammering.
Now
    there was coal in all the stoves,

heat in all the radiators,
and the dome of the Black Tower
was covered with gold once more.
For a moment
the blind forgot their darkness,
the hunchbacks their humps.
For a moment
I didn't have any enemies,
and no one hoped
the old days would return.
Now
Wenceslaus got off his bronze horse
and mixed with the crowd—
no one could tell who he was.
For a moment
you loved me
like you've never loved anyone...
This minute, this second,
sun-bright dry cold, no lies,
dry cold rose-pink,
sky-blue dry cold.
The city of Prague is etched on cut glass
with a diamond point.
If I touch it, it will ring:
gold-edged, clear, white.

FROM SOFIA

I entered Sofia on a spring day, my sweet.
Your native city smelled of linden trees.

It is my fate
to roam the world without you,
what can we do...

In Sofia, trees mean more than walls.
Trees and people blend together here,
                        especially the poplar
                        about to step into my room
                        and sit on the red kilim...

Is Sofia a big city?
Grand avenues don't make a city big, my rose,
but the poets remembered in its monuments.
                        Sofia is a big city...

Evenings here people pour out into the streets:
women and children, young and old,
what laughter, such noise and bustle,
            the buzzing crowd up and down,
        side by side, arm in arm, hand in hand...

Ramazan nights in Istanbul,
people used to promenade this way
                        (that was before your time, Munevver).
No... Those nights are gone...
If I were in Istanbul now,
                        would I think to miss them?
But far from Istanbul
                    I miss everything,
even the visiting room at the Uskudar prison...

I entered Sofia on a spring day, my sweet.
Your native city smelled of linden trees.
Your countrymen welcomed me like you'll never know.
Your native city is my brother's house now.
But even in a brother's house, home can't be forgotten.

Exile is not an easy art to master. . .

24 May 1957
Varna

BOR HOTEL

No way you can sleep nights in Varna,
no way you can sleep:
for the wealth of stars
so close and brilliant,
for the rustle of dead waves on the sand,
of salty weeds
with their pearly shells
and pebbles,
for the sound of a motorboat throbbing like a heart at sea,
for the memories filling my room,
coming from Istanbul,
          passing through the Bosporus,
            and filling my room,
some with green eyes,
some in handcuffs
or holding a handkerchief—
the handkerchief smells of lavender.
No way you can sleep in Varna, my love,
in Varna at the Bor Hotel.

2 June 1957

THE BALCONY

In Kurort-Varna, I look from the balcony
    of the Balkan-Tourist:
the road, trees,
    beyond them sand,
beyond that must be sea and sky—
no,
    neither sea nor sky,
beyond the sand is simply light,
    no end of light. . .
And this smell of roses in the air
burns the nostrils.
I don't see any roses,
but I can tell from the scent
they're all enormous,
    all very red. . .
The Polish tourists flock down to the beach,
blond, pink, half-naked. . .
A swallow spins overhead:
black wings, white breast.
He's not in the least like a bee,
but he's like a bee just the same.
Now you see him, now you don't
as he plunges and soars, giddy
    with his own song. . .
Cucumber soup in a blue bowl.
They brought a cheese pita
—it's as if I'm in Istanbul—
they brought a cheese pita
with sesame seeds, soft and steaming. . .
This summer day in Varna,
all big talk aside,
even for a very sick, very exiled poet
this happiness to be alive.

3 June 1957

THE LAST BUS

Midnight. The last bus.
The conductor cuts me a ticket.
Neither bad news nor a big dinner
          is waiting for me at home.
For me, absence waits.
I approach it without sadness
          or fear.

The great dark is closing in.
Now I can look at the world
          quietly and at peace.
I'm no longer surprised by a friend's treachery,
          a knife concealed in a handshake.
It's useless—the enemy can't provoke me now.
I passed through the forest of idols
          with my axe—
          how easily they all came down.
I put my beliefs to the test once more,
      I'm thankful most of them turned out pure.
I have never been radiant this way,
          never free like this.

The great dark is closing in.
Now I can look at the world
          quietly and at peace.
Suddenly the past comes back
when I'm not looking—
          a word
              a smell
                  the gesture of a hand.
              The word is friendly,
                  the smell beautiful—
                  the hand is in a hand, my love.

The call of memory no longer makes me sad.
I have no complaints about memories.
In fact, I can't complain about anything,
not even about my heart
             aching nonstop like a big tooth.

The great dark is closing in.
Now neither the seer's pride nor the scribe's claptrap.
I'm pouring bowls of light over my head,
I can look at the sun and not be blinded.
And perhaps—what a pity—
             the most beautiful lie
                          will no longer seduce me.
Words can't make me drunk anymore,
neither mine nor anyone else's.
That's how it goes, my rose.
Death now is awfully close.
The world is more beautiful than ever.
The world was my suit of clothes,
                          I started undressing.
I was at the window of a train,
             now I'm at the station.
I was inside the house,
             now I'm at the door—it's open.
I love the guests twice as much.
And the heat is blonder than ever,
             the snow is whiter than ever.

21 July 1957
Prague

CONVERSATION WITH DEAD NEZVAL

Soon after you left
it got cold and snowed.
When that happens, they say the sky
is weeping for the dead.
But that's spring, you know.
On the 13th of April the sun opened up.
Prague suddenly smiled
even there at the cemetery.
Though they still speak of you
almost as if they were praying,
your black-draped photo
stands bright and sunny in the store window.
The weather could turn bad again,
but then we're facing May—
May in Prague, you know,
green, gold-yellow.
When it attacks the streets,
young girls wipe grief clean
like window panes,
and the grief you left us
will vanish like your shadow
from the sidewalks of Prague.
This world... But to tell the truth,
the life-loving, smart,
good-hearted dead
don't want forty days of mourning
or say, "After me the deluge!"
Leaving behind some helpful things
—a few words, a tree, a smile—
each gets up and goes
and does not burden the living
with the darkness of the tomb,
carrying the weight

of his stone all alone.
And because they ask nothing
from the living,
it's as if they aren't dead...
Nezval, I know
you're like that, too—
you, too, are one of the good-hearted,
world-loving, smart
dead of Prague.

20 April 1958
Prague

ELEGY FOR MIKHAIL REFILI

This is the leaf fall of my generation,
most of us won't make winter.

I went crazy, Refili,
when I got the news...
What was I saying...
                    Do you remember, Mikhail...
But you don't have any memory now,
you don't have a nose, mouth, or eyes...
Brother, you're a pile of bones
                    in a Baku cemetery.
What was I saying...
One New Year's Eve in Moscow,
below the decked-out pine tree on our table,
you glowed like a big toy.
Your bright eyes, bald head,
                    respectable belly.
Outside, a snowy forest plunged in darkness.
I looked at you and thought:
        His excellency—pleased as an old barrel of wine,
        hardy as an old wine barrel.
        He'll long outlive me.
        And after I'm gone he'll turn out an article
                or a poem:
        "I met Nazim in Moscow in 1924..."
Really, Mikhail, you could have been a poet,
                you were a professor.
But that's not the point.
The best of the work we do, or the worst,
                lives after us.
Yours was middling, I think.
Mine, too.
        I mean, we don't have the consolation our voices

won't be lost in this world.
For my part, I don't mind.
I've succeeded in living without consolation,
and I'll succeed in dying without it—
                              like you, Refili.

5 June 1958
Prague

THE FAR SOUTH

This year, early fall in the far south,
I steep myself in the sea, sand, and sun,
in trees, in apples like honey.
At night the air smells like ripening grain:
the night sky descends on the hot dusty road,
and I steep myself in stars.

I'm really getting to know
                    the sea, sand, sun, apples, stars.
It's time to go mix
                    with the sea, sand, sun, apples, stars.

8 September 1958
Arhipo Osipovka

138

THE BEES

The bees, like big drops of honey
carrying grapevines to the sun,
came flying out of my youth;
the apples, these heavy apples,
                are also from my youth;
the gold-dust road,
these white pebbles in the stream,
my faith in songs,
my freedom from envy,
the cloudless day, this blue day,
the sea flat on its back, naked and warm,
my longing, these bright teeth and full lips—
they all came to this Caucasian village
like big drops of honey on the legs of bees
out of my youth, the youth I left somewhere
                        before I was through.

13 September 1958
Arhipo Osipovka

THE OLD MAN ON THE SHORE

deep mountains lined up in rows
the pine forest reached to the sea
on the shore an old man lay
stretched out on the pebble beach

and this sun-ripe September day
the distant news of sunken ships
the cool blue of the northeast breeze
caressed the old man's face

his hands were folded on his chest
stubborn and tired like two crabs
the tough hard-shelled triumph
of a journey outlasting time

his salt-wrinkled eyelids
were softly closed
and in the gold-speckled darkness
the old man listened to the roar

the sea the sharp-toothed fish
the flaming dawn
the rocks blooming at the bottom
the nets and the fisherman's home

or maybe the roar came from high
in the pines near the clouds
he knew it would make him dizzy
to look up at them from below

deep mountains lined up in rows
the pine forest reached to the sea
on the shore an old man lay
stretched out on the pebble beach

24 September 1958
Pitsunda

OPTIMISTIC MAN

as a child he never plucked the wings off flies
he didn't tie tin cans to cats' tails
or lock beetles in matchboxes
or stomp anthills
he grew up
and all those things were done to him
I was at his bedside when he died
he said read me a poem
about the sun and the sea
about nuclear reactors and satellites
about the greatness of humanity

6 December 1958
Baku

THIS JOURNEY

We open doors,
close doors,
pass through doors,
and reach at the end of our only journey
                              no city,
                              no harbor—
the train derails,
the ship sinks
the plane crashes.
The map is drawn on ice.
But if I could
        begin this journey all over again,
                              I would.

1958
Leningrad

THE ICEBREAKER

The icebreaker leads the way,
our boat shudders in its wake.
I watch from my cabin porthole,
the sea is frozen solid white.
I come from Istanbul—
I grew up by the warm, salt sea.
We like our colors, light, and life clear-cut.
We have poppy fields,
streets,
covered bazaars,
and pigeons,
but the liveliest of all is our sea.
Our sea is blue-green,
more impatient than a northeaster
       and quicker than dolphins.
Where I come from, summer noons
    when not a leaf is moving,
      it still moves,
        endlessly
          trembling.
We never forget its fragrance.
I watch from my cabin porthole,
the sea is frozen
        solid
          white.
I watch,
    devastated.

1959
Leningrad-Stockholm

WAITRESS

One of the waitresses
                    at Berlin's Astoria Restaurant
                    was a jewel of a girl.
She'd smile at me across her heavy trays.
She looked like the girls of the country I've lost.
Sometimes she had dark circles under her eyes—
                                        I don't know why.
I never got to sit
                at one of her tables.

He never once sat at one of my tables.
He was an old man.
And he must have been sick—
                    he was on a special diet.
He could gaze at my face so sadly,
                    but he couldn't speak German.
For three months he came in for three meals a day,
then he disappeared.
Maybe he went back to his country,
                    maybe he died before he could.

23 July 1959

BAKU AT NIGHT

Reaching down to the starless heavy sea
in the pitch-black night,
Baku is a sunny wheatfield.
High above on a hill,
grains of light hit my face by the handfuls,
and the music in the air flows like the Bosporus.
High above on a hill,
my heart goes out like a raft

              into the endless absence,
              beyond memory
              down to the starless heavy sea
              in the pitch dark.

February 1960

EARLY LIGHT

The telegraph poles in the early light,
                    the road.
The dresser mirror brightening,
                    the table,
                              slippers.
Things recognize each other once again.
In our room the early light unfolds like a sail,
the cool air is diamond-blue.
The stars pale—
far away,
          pebbles bleach white deep in the sky's stream.
My rose is sleeping,
      her head on the enormous feather pillow.
Her hands on the quilt look like two white tulips.
Birds start singing in her hair.
The city in the early light:
the trees are wet, the smokestacks hot.
The first footsteps caressing the asphalt
      pass through our room,
            the hum of the first engine,
                  the first laugh,
                  the first curse.
The steamed-up glass case of the pastry cart,
the driver in boots entering the dairy store,
the neighbors' crying child,
the dove in the blue poster,
the manikin with yellow shoes
            in the window,
and Chinese fans of sandalwood
and her full red lips
and the happiest and freshest of awakenings
      all pass through our room in the early light.
I turn on the radio:

metals with giant names mix with giant numbers,
oil wells race with cornfields.
The shepherd who got the Lenin Medal
   (I saw his picture on the front page,
     his thick mustache black and drooping)
speaks shyly like a young girl.
Then the news from around the world.
Then, as Sputnik III
    circles the earth for the 8878th time
      at six this morning,
my rose opens her big eyes on the pillow.
They're still like smoky mountain lakes:
blue fish flicker in them,
green pines rise in their depths.
They look out deep and flat.
The last of her dreams flashes in the early morning.
I'm illuminated,
I know myself once more.
I'm recklessly happy
   and a bit embarrassed,
     but just a little bit.
In the early morning the light in our room
    is like a sail
      spread for a voyage.
My rose gets out of bed naked like an apricot.
In the early light the bed is snow-white
    like the dove in the blue poster.

February 1960
Kislovodsk

THE CUCUMBER

to Ekber Babayev

The snow is knee-deep in the courtyard
and still coming down hard:
it hasn't let up all morning.
We're in the kitchen.
On the table, on the oilcloth, spring—
on the table there's a very tender young cucumber,
                              pebbly and fresh as a daisy.
We're sitting around the table staring at it.
It softly lights up our faces,
and the very air smells fresh.
We're sitting around the table staring at it,
amazed
            thoughtful
                        optimistic.
We're as if in a dream.
On the table, on the oilcloth, hope—
on the table, beautiful days,
a cloud seeded with a green sun,
an emerald crowd impatient and on its way,
loves blooming openly—
on the table, there on the oilcloth, a very tender young
                                          cucumber,
                     pebbly and fresh as a daisy.
The snow is knee-deep in the courtyard
and coming down hard.
It hasn't let up all morning.

March 1960
Moscow

MY WOMAN

My woman came with me as far as Brest,
she got off the train and stayed on the platform,
she grew smaller and smaller,
she became a kernel of wheat in the infinite blue,
then all I could see were the tracks.

Then she called out from Poland, but I couldn't answer,
I couldn't ask, "Where are you, my rose, where are you?"
"Come," she said, but I couldn't reach her,
the train was going like it would never stop,
I was choking with grief.

Then patches of snow were rotting on sandy earth,
and suddenly I knew my woman was watching:
"Did you forget me," she asked, "did you forget me?"
Spring was marching with muddy bare feet on the sky.

Then stars lighted on the telegraph wires,
darkness lashed the train like rain,
my woman stood under the telegraph poles,
her heart pounding as if she were in my arms,
the poles kept disappearing, she didn't move,
the train was going like it would never stop,
I was choking with grief.

Then suddenly I knew I'd been on that train for years
—I'm still amazed at how or why I knew it—
and always singing the same great song of hope,
I'm forever leaving the cities and women I love,
and carrying my losses like wounds opening inside me,
I'm getting closer, closer to somewhere.

March 1960
Mediterranean Sea

VERA WAKING

the chairs are asleep on their feet
                   the same as the table
the rug lies stretched out on its back
                    clutching its design
the mirror is sleeping
the eyes of the windows are closed tight
the balcony sleeps with its legs dangling over the edge
on the opposite roof the chimneys are sleeping
                   the same as the acacias on the sidewalk
the cloud sleeps
          with a star on its chest
the light is asleep indoors and out
you woke up my rose
the chairs awoke
      and scrambled from corner to corner
               the same as the table
the rug sat up straight
           slowly unfolding its colors
like a lake at sunrise the mirror awakened
the windows opened their big blue eyes
the balcony woke up
          and pulled its legs out of the air
on the opposite roof the chimneys smoked
the acacias on the sidewalk broke into song
the cloud woke up
          and tossed the star on its chest into our room
the light woke up indoors and out
               flooding your hair
                  it slipped through your fingers
    and embraced your naked waist those white feet of yours

May 1960
Moscow

STRAW-BLOND

to Vera Tulyakova,
with my deep respect

I

at dawn the express entered the station unannounced
it was covered with snow
I stood on the platform my coat collar raised
the platform was empty
a sleeper window stopped in front of me
its curtains were parted
a young woman slept in the lower berth in the twilight
her hair straw-blond eyelashes blue
and her full red lips looked spoiled and pouting
I didn't see who was sleeping in the upper berth
unannounced the express slipped out of the station
I don't know where it came from or where it was going
I watched it leave
I was sleeping in the upper berth
                              in the Bristol Hotel in Warsaw
I hadn't slept so soundly in years
and yet my bed was wooden and narrow
a young woman slept in another bed
her hair straw-blond eyelashes blue
her white neck long and smooth
she hadn't slept so soundly in years
and yet her bed was wooden and narrow
time sped on we were nearing midnight
we hadn't slept so soundly in years
and yet our beds were wooden and narrow
I'm coming down the stairs from the fourth floor
the elevator is out again
inside mirrors I'm coming down the stairs

I could be twenty I could be a hundred
time sped on I was nearing midnight
on the third floor a woman was laughing behind a door
        a sad rose slowly opened in my right hand
I met a Cuban ballerina at the snowy windows on the second floor
she flashed past my forehead like a fresh dark flame
the poet Nicolas Guillen went back to Havana long ago
for years we sat in the hotel lobbies of Europe and Asia
        drinking the loss of our cities drop by drop
two things are forgotten only with death
the face of our mothers and the face of our cities
wood barges swim into the wind early mornings in winter
        like old rowboats that have cut themselves loose
and in the ashes of a brazier
        my big Istanbul wakes up from sleep
two things are forgotten only with death
the doorman saw me off his cloak sinking into the night
I walked into the icy wind and neon
time sped on I was nearing midnight
they came upon me suddenly
it was light as day but no one else saw
a squad of them
they had jackboots pants coats
arms swastikas on their arms
hands automatics in their hands
they had shoulders helmets on their shoulders but no heads
between their shoulders and their helmets nothing
they even had collars and necks but no heads
they were the soldiers whose deaths are not mourned
I walked on
you could see their fear animal fear
I can't say it showed in their eyes
they didn't have heads to have eyes
you could see their fear animal fear
it showed in their boots

can boots show fear
theirs did
in their fear they opened fire
they fired nonstop at all buildings all vehicles all living things
at every sound the least movement
they even fired at a poster of blue fish on Chopin Street
but not so much as a piece of plaster fell or a window broke
and no one but me heard the shots
the dead even an SS squad the dead can't kill
the dead kill by coming back as worms inside the apple
but you could see their fear animal fear
wasn't this city killed before they were
weren't the bones of this city broken one by one and its skin flayed
weren't bookcovers made from its skin soap from its oil rope
    from its hair
but there it was standing before them
like a hot loaf of bread in the icy night wind
time sped on I was nearing midnight
on Belvedere road I thought of the Poles
they dance a heroic mazurka through history
on Belvedere road I thought of the Poles
in this palace they gave me my first and maybe last medal
the master of ceremonies opened the gilded white door
I entered the hall with a young woman
her hair straw-blond eyelashes blue
and no one was there but us two
plus the aquarelles and delicate chairs and sofas like doll furniture
and you became
            a blue-tinted pastel or a porcelain doll
or maybe a spark from my dream landed on my chest
you slept in the lower berth in the twilight
your white neck long and smooth
you hadn't slept so soundly in years
and here in the Caprice Bar in Cracow
time speeds on we're nearing midnight

separation was on the table between the coffee cup and my glass
you put it there
it was the water at the bottom of a stone well
I lean over and see
an old man dimly smiling at a cloud
I call out
the echoes of my voice return without you
separation was in the cigarette package on the table
the waiter with glasses brought it but you ordered it
it was smoke curling in your eyes
it was at the end of your cigarette
and in your hand waiting to say goodbye
separation was on the table where you rested your elbow
it was in what went through your mind
             in what you hid from me and what you didn't
separation was in your calm
             in your trust in me
it was in your great fear
to fall in love with someone out of the blue as if your door burst open
actually you love me and don't know it
separation was in your not knowing
separation was free of gravity weightless I can't say like a feather
    even a feather weighs something separation was weightless
    but it was there
time speeds on midnight approaches
we walked in the shadow of medieval walls reaching the stars
time sped backward
the echoes of our steps returned like scrawny yellow dogs
they ran behind us and in front
the devil roams Jagiellonian University
digging his nails into the stones
he's out to sabotage the astrolabe Copernicus got from the Arabs
and in the market place under the Cloth Arcade
he's with the Catholic students dancing to rock 'n' roll
time speeds on midnight approaches

the red glow of Nowa Huta lights the clouds
there young workers from the villages cast their souls along with iron
burning into new molds
and casting souls is a thousand times harder than casting iron
the trumpeter who tells the hours in the bell tower of St. Mary's
    Church
sounded midnight
his call rose out of the Middle Ages
                    warned the city of the enemy's approach
and was cut off by an arrow through the throat
the herald died at peace
and I thought of the pain
of dying before announcing the enemy's approach
time speeds on midnight recedes
like a ferry landing gone dark
at dawn the express entered the station unannounced
Prague was all rain
it was an inlaid-silver chest at the bottom of a lake
I opened it
inside a young woman slept among glass birds
her hair straw-blond eyelashes blue
she hadn't slept so soundly in years
I closed the chest and put it on the baggage car
unannounced the express slipped out of the station
arms hanging at my sides I watched it leave
Prague was all rain
you aren't here
you're sleeping in the lower berth in the twilight
the upper berth is empty
you aren't here
one of the world's most beautiful cities is empty
like a glove pulled off your hand
it went dark like mirrors that no longer see you
the waters of the Vltava disappear under bridges like lost nights
the streets are all empty

in all the windows the curtains are drawn
the streetcars go by all empty
        they don't even have conductors or drivers
the coffeehouses are empty
        bars and restaurants too
the store windows are empty
        no cloth no crystal no meat no wine
        not a book not a box of candy not a carnation
and in this loneliness enfolding the city like fog an old man try-
   ing to shake off the sadness of age made ten times worse by
   loneliness throws bread to the gulls from Legionnaires Bridge
        dipping each piece in the blood
        of his too-young heart
I want to catch the minutes
the gold dust of their speed stays on my fingers
a woman sleeps in the lower berth in the sleeper
she hasn't slept so soundly in years
her hair straw-blond eyelashes blue
her hands candles in silver candlesticks
I can't see who's sleeping in the upper berth
if anyone is sleeping there it isn't me
maybe the upper berth is empty
maybe Moscow is in the upper berth
fog has settled over Poland
        over Brest too
for two days now planes can't land or take off
but the trains come and go they go through hollowed-out eyes
since Berlin I was alone in the compartment
the next morning I woke to sun on snowy fields
in the dining car I drank a kind of *ayran* called kefir
the waitress recognized me
she'd seen two of my plays in Moscow
a young woman met me at the station
her waist narrower than an ant's
her hair straw-blond eyelashes blue

I took her hand and we walked
we walked in the sun cracking the snow
spring came early that year
those days they flew news to the evening star
Moscow was happy I was happy we were happy
suddenly I lost you in Mayakovsky Square I lost you suddenly no
    not suddenly because I first lost the warmth of your hand in
    mine then the soft weight of your hand in my palm and then
    your hand
and separation had set in long ago at the first touch of our fingers
but I still lost you suddenly
on the sea of asphalt I stopped the cars and looked inside no you
the boulevards all under snow
yours not among the footprints
I know your footprints in boots shoes stockings bare
I asked the guards
didn't you see
if she took off her gloves you couldn't miss her hands
they're like candles in silver candlesticks
the guards answered very politely
we didn't see
a tugboat breasts the current at Seraglio Point in Istanbul
behind it three barges
awk awk the sea gulls go awk awk
I called out to the barges from Red Square I didn't call to the
    tugboat captain because he wouldn't have heard me over the
    roar of his engine besides he was tired and his coat had no
    buttons
I called out to the barges from Red Square
we didn't see
I stood I'm standing in all the lines in all the streets of Moscow
and I'm asking just the women
old women quiet and patient with smiling faces under wool babushkas
young women rosy-cheeked and straight-nosed in green velvet hats
and young girls very clean and firm and elegant too

maybe there are frightful old women weary young women and
    sloppy girls
                but who cares about them
women spot beauty before men do and they don't forget it
didn't you see
her hair straw-blond eyelashes blue
her black coat has a white collar and big pearl buttons
she got it in Prague
we didn't see
I'm racing the minutes now they're ahead now me
when they're ahead I'm scared I'll lose sight
of their disappearing red lights
when I'm ahead their headlights throw my shadow on the road
    my shadow races ahead of me suddenly I'm afraid I'll lose
    sight of my shadow
I go into theaters concerts movies
I didn't try the Bolshoi you don't like tonight's opera
I went into Fisherman's Bar in Istanbul and sat talking sweetly
    with Sait Faik I was out of prison a month his liver was hurt-
    ing and the world was beautiful
I go into restaurants with brassy orchestras famous bands
I ask gold-braided doormen and aloof tip-loving waiters
hatcheck girls and the neighborhood watchman
we didn't see
the clock tower of the Strastnoi Monastery rang midnight
actually both tower and monastery were torn down long ago
they're building the city's biggest movie house there
that's where I met my nineteenth year
we recognized each other right away
yet we hadn't seen each other not even photos
we still recognized each other right away we weren't surprised
    we tried to shake hands
but our hands couldn't touch forty years of time stood between us
a North Sea frozen and endless
and it started snowing in Strastnoi now Pushkin Square

I'm cold especially my hands and feet
yet I have wool socks and fur-lined boots and gloves
he's the one without socks his feet wrapped in rags inside old
    boots his hands bare
the world is the taste of a green apple in his mouth
the feel of a fourteen-year-old girl's breasts in his hands
songs go for miles and miles in his eyes death measures a hand's-span
and he has no idea what all will happen to him
only I know what will happen
because I believed everything he believes
I loved all the women he'll love
I wrote all the poems he'll write
I stayed in all the prisons he'll stay in
I passed through all the cities he will visit
I suffered all his illnesses
I slept all his nights dreamed all his dreams
I lost all that he will lose
her hair straw-blond eyelashes blue
her black coat has a white collar and big pearl buttons
I didn't see

II

my nineteenth year crosses Beyazit Square comes out on Red Square
and goes down to Concorde I meet Abidin and we talk squares
the day before yesterday Gagarin circled the biggest square of all
    and returned
Titov too will go around and come back seventeen-and-a-half
    times even but I don't know about it yet
I talk spaces and shapes with Abidin in my attic hotel room
and the Seine flows on both sides of Notre Dame
from my window at night I see the Seine as a sliver of moonlight
    on the wharf of the stars
and a young woman sleeps in my attic room

mixed with the chimneys of the Paris roofs
she hasn't slept so soundly in years
her straw-blond hair curled her blue eyelashes like clouds on her face
with Abidin I discuss the space and shape of the atom's seed
we speak of Rumi whirling in space
Abidin paints the colors of unlimited speed
I eat up the colors like fruit
and Matisse is a fruitpeddler he sells the fruits of the cosmos
like our Abidin and Avni and Levni
and the spaces shapes and colors seen by microscopes and rocket
    portholes
and their poets painters and musicians
in the space of one-fifty by sixty Abidin paints the surge forward
    the way I can see and catch fish in water that's how I see and
    catch the bright moments flowing on Abidin's canvas
and the Seine is like a sliver of moonlight
a young woman sleeps in a sliver of moonlight
how many times have I lost her how many times have I found
    her and how many more times will I lose her and find her
that's the way it is girl that's how it is I dropped part of my life
    into the Seine from St. Michel Bridge
one morning in drizzling light that part will catch Monsieur Dupont's
    fishline
Monsieur Dupont will pull it out of the water along with the blue
    picture of Paris he won't make anything of my life it won't be
    like a fish or a shoe
Monsieur Dupont will throw it back along with the blue picture of Paris
the picture will stay where it was
the part of my life will flow with the Seine into the great cemetery
    of rivers
I woke to the rustle of blood in my veins
my fingers weightless
my fingers and toes about to snap off take to the air and circle
    lazily overhead
no right and left or up and down

I should ask Abidin to paint the student shot in Beyazit Square
      and comrade Gagarin and comrade Titov whose name fame
      or face I don't know yet and those to come after him and the
      young woman asleep in the attic
I got back from Cuba this morning
in the space that is Cuba six million people whites blacks yellows
      mulattoes are planting a bright seed the seed of seeds joyously
can you paint happiness Abidin
but without taking the easy way out
not the angel-faced mother nursing her rosy-cheeked baby
nor the apples on white cloth
nor the goldfish darting among aquarium bubbles
can you paint happiness Abidin
can you paint Cuba in midsummer 1961
master can you paint *Praise be praise be I saw the day I could die now
      and not be sorry*
can you paint *What a pity what a pity I could have been born in
      Havana this morning*
I saw a hand 150 kilometers east of Havana close to the sea
I saw a hand on a wall
the wall was an open song
the hand caressed the wall
the hand was six months old and stroked its mother's neck
the hand was seventeen years old and caressed Maria's breasts
its palm was calloused and smelled of the Caribbean
it was twenty and stroked the neck of its six-month-old son
the hand was twenty-five and had forgotten how to caress
the hand was thirty and I saw it on a wall near the sea 150
      kilometers east of Havana caressing a wall
you draw hands Abidin those of our laborers and ironworkers
      draw with charcoal the hand of the Cuban fisherman Nicolas
who on the wall of the shiny house he got from the cooperative
      rediscovered caressing and won't forget it again
a big hand
a sea turtle of a hand

a hand that didn't believe it could caress an open wall
a hand that now believes in all joys
a sunny salty sacred hand
the hand of hopes that sprout green and sweeten with the speed
    of sugar cane in earth fertile as Fidel's words
one of the hands in Cuba in 1961 that plant houses like colorful
    cool trees and trees like very comfortable houses
one of the hands preparing to pour steel
the hand that makes songs of machine guns and machine guns
    of songs
the hand of freedom without lies
the hand Fidel shook
the hand that writes the word *freedom* with the first pencil and
    paper of its life
when they say the word *freedom* the Cubans' mouths water
as if they were slicing a honey of a melon
and the men's eyes gleam
and the girls melt when their lips touch the word *freedom*
and the old people draw from the well their sweetest memories
    and slowly sip them
can you paint happiness Abidin
can you paint freedom the kind without lies
night is falling in Paris
Notre Dame lit up like an orange lamp and went out
and in Paris all the stones old and new lit up like orange lamps
    and went out
I think of our crafts the business of poetry painting music and so on
I think and I know
a great river flows from the time the first human hand drew the
    first bison in the first cave
then all streams run into it with their new fish new water-grasses
    new tastes and it alone flows endlessly and never dries up
I've heard there's a chestnut tree in Paris
the first of the Paris chestnuts the granddaddy of them all
it came from Istanbul the hills of the Bosporus and settled in Paris

I don't know if it's still standing it would be about two hundred
  years old
I wish I could go shake its hand
I wish we could go lie in its shade the people who make the
  paper for this book who set its type who print its drawings
  those who sell this book in their stores who pay money and
  buy it who buy it and look at it and Abidin and me too plus
  the straw-blond trouble of my life

1961

UNTITLED

he was stone bronze plaster and paper anywhere from two
centimeters to seven meters
    in all the city squares we were under his stone bronze
plaster and paper boots
    in parks his stone bronze plaster and paper shadow darkened
our trees
    his stone bronze plaster and paper mustache got in our soup
in restaurants
    in our rooms we were under his stone bronze plaster and
paper eyes
    he vanished one morning
            his boots disappeared from our squares
                his shadow from our trees
                    his mustache from our soup
                        his eyes from our rooms
    and the weight of thousands of tons of stone bronze plaster
and paper was lifted off our backs

1961
Moscow

AUTOBIOGRAPHY

I was born in 1902
I never once went back to my birthplace
I don't like to turn back
at three I served as a pasha's grandson in Aleppo
at nineteen as a student at Moscow Communist University
at forty-nine I was back in Moscow as the Tcheka Party's guest
and I've been a poet since I was fourteen
some people know all about plants some about fish
                                        I know separation
some people know the names of the stars by heart
                                        I recite absences
I've slept in prisons and in grand hotels
I've known hunger even a hunger strike and there's almost no food
    I haven't tasted
at thirty they wanted to hang me
at forty-eight to give me the Peace Prize
                                        which they did
at thirty-six I covered four square meters of concrete in half a year
at fifty-nine I flew from Prague to Havana in eighteen hours
I never saw Lenin I stood watch at his coffin in '24
in '61 the tomb I visit is his books
they tried to tear me away from my party
                                        it didn't work
nor was I crushed under falling idols
in '51 I sailed with a young friend into the teeth of death
in '52 I spent four months flat on my back with a broken heart
    waiting to die
I was jealous of the women I loved
I didn't envy Charlie Chaplin one bit
I deceived my women
I never talked behind my friends' backs
I drank but not every day
I earned my bread money honestly what happiness

out of embarrassment for others I lied
I lied so as not to hurt someone else
                    but I also lied for no reason at all
I've ridden in trains planes and cars
most people don't get the chance
I went to the opera
            most people haven't even heard of the opera
and since '21 I haven't gone to the places most people visit
            mosques churches temples synagogues sorcerers
            but I've had my coffee grounds read
my writings are published in thirty or forty languages
            in my Turkey in my Turkish they're banned
cancer hasn't caught up with me yet
and nothing says it will
I'll never be a prime minister or anything like that
and I wouldn't want such a life
nor did I go to war
or burrow in bomb shelters in the bottom of the night
and I never had to take to the road under diving planes
but I fell in love at almost sixty
in short comrades
even if today in Berlin I'm croaking of grief
                I can say I've lived like a human being
and who knows
                how much longer I'll live
                what else will happen to me

*This autobiography was written
in East Berlin on 11 September 1961*

THINGS I DIDN'T KNOW I LOVED

it's 1962 March 28th
I'm sitting by the window on the Prague-Berlin train
night is falling
I never knew I liked
night descending like a tired bird on a smoky wet plain
I don't like
comparing nightfall to a tired bird

I didn't know I loved the earth
can someone who hasn't worked the earth love it
I've never worked the earth
it must be my only Platonic love

and here I've loved rivers all this time
whether motionless like this they curl skirting the hills
European hills crowned with chateaus
or whether stretched out flat as far as the eye can see
I know you can't wash in the same river even once
I know the river will bring new lights you'll never see
I know we live slightly longer than a horse but not nearly as long
      as a crow
I know this has troubled people before
                              and will trouble those after me
I know all this has been said a thousand times before
                        and will be said after me

I didn't know I loved the sky
cloudy or clear
the blue vault Andrei studied on his back at Borodino
in prison I translated both volumes of *War and Peace* into Turkish
I hear voices
not from the blue vault but from the yard
the guards are beating someone again

I didn't know I loved trees
bare beeches near Moscow in Peredelkino
they come upon me in winter noble and modest
beeches are Russian the way poplars are Turkish
"the poplars of Izmir
losing their leaves. . .
they call me The Knife. . .
                    lover like a young tree. . .
I blow stately mansions sky-high"
in the Ilgaz woods in 1920 I tied an embroidered linen handkerchief
                              to a pine bough for luck

I never knew I loved roads
even the asphalt kind
Vera's behind the wheel we're driving from Moscow to the Crimea
                              Koktebele
                    formerly "Goktepé ili" in Turkish
the two of us inside a closed box
the world flows past on both sides distant and mute
I was never so close to anyone in my life
bandits stopped me on the red road between Bolu and Geredé
                              when I was eighteen
apart from my life I didn't have anything in the wagon they could take
and at eighteen our lives are what we value least
I've written this somewhere before
wading through a dark muddy street I'm going to the shadow play
Ramazan night
a paper lantern leading the way
maybe nothing like this ever happened
maybe I read it somewhere an eight-year-old boy
                              going to the shadow play
Ramazan night in Istanbul holding his grandfather's hand
   his grandfather has on a fez and is wearing the fur coat
      with a sable collar over his robe
   and there's a lantern in the servant's hand
   and I can't contain myself for joy

flowers come to mind for some reason
poppies cactuses jonquils
in the jonquil garden in Kadikoy Istanbul I kissed Marika
fresh almonds on her breath
I was seventeen
my heart on a swing touched the sky
I didn't know I loved flowers
friends sent me three red carnations in prison

I just remembered the stars
I love them too
whether I'm floored watching them from below
or whether I'm flying at their side

I have some questions for the cosmonauts
were the stars much bigger
did they look like huge jewels on black velvet
                              or apricots on orange
did you feel proud to get closer to the stars
I saw color photos of the cosmos in *Ogonek* magazine now don't
    be upset comrades but nonfigurative shall we say or abstract
    well some of them looked just like such paintings which is to
    say they were terribly figurative and concrete
my heart was in my mouth looking at them
they are our endless desire to grasp things
seeing them I could even think of death and not feel at all sad
I never knew I loved the cosmos

snow flashes in front of my eyes
both heavy wet steady snow and the dry whirling kind
I didn't know I liked snow

I never knew I loved the sun
even when setting cherry-red as now
in Istanbul too it sometimes sets in postcard colors
but you aren't about to paint it that way

I didn't know I loved the sea
                              except the Sea of Azov
or how much

I didn't know I loved clouds
whether I'm under or up above them
whether they look like giants or shaggy white beasts

moonlight the falsest the most languid the most petit-bourgeois
strikes me
I like it

I didn't know I liked rain
whether it falls like a fine net or splatters against the glass my
    heart leaves me tangled up in a net or trapped inside a drop
    and takes off for uncharted countries I didn't know I loved
    rain but why did I suddenly discover all these passions sitting
    by the window on the Prague-Berlin train
is it because I lit my sixth cigarette
one alone could kill me
is it because I'm half dead from thinking about someone back in
    Moscow
her hair straw-blond eyelashes blue

the train plunges on through the pitch-black night
I never knew I liked the night pitch-black
sparks fly from the engine
I didn't know I loved sparks
I didn't know I loved so many things and I had to wait until sixty
    to find it out sitting by the window on the Prague-Berlin train
    watching the world disappear as if on a journey of no return

19 April 1962
Moscow

I STEPPED OUT OF MY THOUGHTS OF DEATH

I stepped out of my thoughts of death
and put on the June leaves of the boulevards
those of May after all were too young for me
a whole summer waits for me a city summer with its hot stones
    and asphalt
its ice-cold pop ice cream sweaty movie houses thick-voiced
    actors from the provinces
with its taxis that suddenly vanish on big soccer days
and its trees that turn to paper under the lights of the
    Hermitage garden
and maybe with Mexican songs or tom-toms from Ghana
and the poems I'll read on the balcony
and with your hair cut a little shorter
a city summer is waiting for me
I put on the June leaves of the boulevards
I stepped out of my thoughts of death

24 May 1962

I'M GETTING USED TO GROWING OLD

I'm getting used to growing old,
the hardest art in the world—
knocking on doors for the last time,
endless separation.
The hours run and run and run. . .
I want to understand at the cost of losing faith.
I tried to tell you something, and I couldn't.
The world tastes like an early morning cigarette:
death has sent me its loneliness first.
I envy those who don't even know they're growing old,
they're so buried in their work.

12 January 1963

BERLIN LETTERS

1
Berlin is bright and sunny.
March 8, 1963.
On the phone this morning
I forgot to wish you a happy holiday.
When I hear your voice, I forget the world.
Many happy returns, my beauty.

8 March 1963

2
In four days I'll be in Moscow.
This separation will also end, thank God, and I'll return.
I'll leave it behind like a rainy road.
New separations will follow,
I'll dip into new wells,
I'll take off for somewhere and come back.
I'll run, breathless, to new returns.
Then neither Berlin nor Tanganyika—
nowhere, I'll go nowhere.
I won't return—no boat, no train, no plane.
No letters will come from me, no telegrams.
And I won't call you on the phone.
You won't laugh softly at my voice
or get any more news from me—
you'll be left all alone.
In four days I'll be in Moscow.
Berlin is bright and sunny.
On the phone you said
it's spring in Moscow.
This separation will also end, thank God, and I'll return.
But inside me is the night of our great separation,

your pain of being without me,
your loneliness.
Loneliness—the tasteless bread of memories,
   their call to distance.
Maybe three months, maybe three years,
loneliness will shadow you.
In four days I'll be in Moscow.
On the phone you said
it's spring in Moscow.

8 April 1963

3
I'll be at your side in five hours.
In Berlin
       sunlight, birds singing
           —it rained this morning—
             streetcars,
               and time
                  fill my hotel room.
Time doesn't move,
it's frozen solid.
You could hang it on a hanger
or cut it with a knife.
It's like being in prison,
       where time
            is the cruelest guard.
I'll be at the airport in two hours.
In five, in your blue.
Freedom five hours away.
Statues of whoever invented airplanes
should grace the hotel rooms of all returns.

12 April 1963

MY FUNERAL

Will my funeral start out from our courtyard?
How will you get me down from the third floor?
The coffin won't fit in the elevator,
and the stairs are awfully narrow.

Maybe there'll be sun knee-deep in the yard, and pigeons,
maybe snow filled with the cries of children,
maybe rain with its wet asphalt.
And the trash cans will stand in the courtyard as always.

If, as is the custom here, I'm put in the truck face open,
a pigeon might drop something on my forehead: it's good luck.
Band or no band, the children will come up to me—
they're curious about the dead.

Our kitchen window will watch me leave.
Our balcony will see me off with the wash on the line.
In this yard I was happier than you'll ever know.
Neighbors, I wish you all long lives.

April 1963
Moscow

NOTES

GIOCONDA AND SI-YA-U. Si-Ya-U: Hsiao San (b. 1896), Chinese revolutionary and man of letters. Hikmet met him in Moscow in 1922 and believed he had been executed in the bloody 1927 crackdown on Shanghai radicals after returning to China via Paris in 1924, when the Mona Lisa did in fact disappear from the Louvre. The two friends were reunited in Vienna in 1951 and traveled to Peking together in 1952. Translated into Chinese, this poem was later burned—along with Hsiao's own works—in the Cultural Revolution.

ON DEATH AGAIN. Pirayé: Hikmet's second wife.

ISTANBUL HOUSE OF DETENTION. Bedreddin: Sheik Bedreddin (1359?–1420), Turkish scholar, mystic, and early socialist executed for leading an uprising of Turkish, Greek, and Jewish peasants against the Ottoman Sultan. Sinan (1489–1588): Ottoman architect. Yunus Emré (1250–1320): Turkish folk poet. Sakarya: river in central Anatolia and the site of a major battle in the Turkish War of Independence.

LETTERS FROM CHANKIRI PRISON. Ghazali (d. 1534): Ottoman poet.

9-10 P.M. POEMS. The title of this sequence derives from the hour before lights out in prison, when Hikmet promised his wife to think and write only of her.

ON IBRAHIM BALABAN'S "SPRING PAINTING." Ibrahim Balaban (b. 1921): Turkish artist whom Hikmet met and educated in prison.

TO LYDIA IVANNA. Kostya: Konstantin Simonov (b. 1915), Russian poet. Memet: Hikmet's son, born in 1951.

FROM SOFIA. Munevver: Hikmet's third wife. Now living in Paris, she has translated much of his work into French.

CONVERSATION WITH DEAD NEZVAL. Nezval: Vitezslav Nezval (1900–1958), Czech poet.

THE CUCUMBER. Ekber Babayev: Russian translator, editor, and critic.

VERA WAKING. Vera: Vera Tulyakova, Hikmet's fourth wife.

STRAW-BLOND. Sait Faik (1906–1954): Turkish fiction writer. Abidin: Adibin Dino (b. 1913), Turkish artist who has illustrated many of Hikmet's books. Rumi (1207–1273): Sufi mystic poet who founded in Turkey the order of whirling dervishes. Avni: Avni Arbash (b. 1919), Turkish artist living in Paris. Levni (d. 1732): Ottoman miniaturist.